# How to Use This Book

## Look for these special features in this book:

**SIDEBARS**, **CHARTS**, **GRAPHS**, and original **MAPS** expand your understanding of what's being discussed—and also make useful sources for classroom reports.

**FAQs** answer common **F**requently **A**sked **Q**uestions about people, places, and things.

**WOW FACTORS** offer "Who knew?" facts to keep you thinking.

**TRAVEL GUIDE** gives you tips on exploring the state—either in person or right from your chair!

**PROJECT ROOM** provides fun ideas for school assignments and incredible research projects. Plus, there's a guide to primary sources—what they are and how to cite them.

Please note: All statistics are as up-to-date as possible at the time of publication.

Consultants: Cathy Connor, Associate Professor of Geology, Department of Natural Sciences, University of Alaska Southeast; Stephen Haycox, Professor of History, University of Alaska–Anchorage; William Loren Katz; Dagmar Phillips, 2006 Alaska Studies Teacher of the Year (West High School, Anchorage) (Governor's Award)

Book production by The Design Lab

Library of Congress Cataloging-in-Publication Data
Orr, Tamra.
 Alaska / Tamra B. Orr.
    p. cm.—(America the beautiful. Third series)
 Includes bibliographical references and index.
  ISBN-13: 978-0-531-18569-8
  ISBN-10: 0-531-18569-9
  1. Alaska—Juvenile literature. I. Title. II. Series.
 F904.3.O77 2008
 979.8—dc22                          2007022220

# Alaska

BY TAMRA B. ORR

Third Series

Children's Press®
An Imprint of Scholastic Inc.
New York ★ Toronto ★ London ★ Auckland ★ Sydney
Mexico City ★ New Delhi ★ Hong Kong
Danbury, Connecticut

# CONTENTS

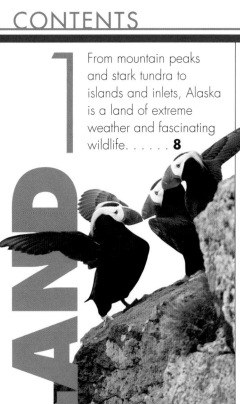

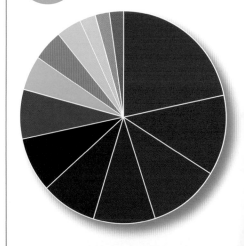

# 4
## GROWTH AND CHANGE

The Alaska Territory grows as gold is discovered and thousands of people seek their fortunes. . . . **44**

# MORE MODERN TIMES

## 5

World War II takes a toll, a pipeline is built, and the state is shaken by a huge earthquake. . . . . . . **58**

# 9 TRAVEL GUIDE

From breathtaking natural scenery to intriguing museums, Alaska has something to offer every visitor to the state. . . . . . . **108**

**PROJECT ROOM**

★

ARCTIC

BARROW

BEAUFORT
SEA

Colville

Brooks Range

Arctic National
Wildlife Refuge

RUSSIA

BERING STRAIT

Yukon

CANADA

Denali

Gold Rush Town

NOME

ALASKA

FAIRBANKS

Alaska Native
Heritage
Center

Tanana

Iditarod

Alaska Zoo

ANCHORAGE

VALDEZ

Klondike Gold
Rush National
Historic Park

SKAGWAY

Alaska State
Capitol

BERING
SEA

Lake
Iliamna

SEWARD

JUNEAU

The Valley of
Ten Thousand
Smokes

BRISTOL
BAY

Alaska SeaLife
Center

SITKA

KODIAK

Aleutian Islands

UNALASKA

GULF OF ALASKA

Sitka National
Historical Park

Aleutian Islands

UNALASKA

PACIFIC
OCEAN

0       200
Miles

# Welcome to Alaska!

## HOW DID ALASKA GET ITS NAME?

The homeland of the Aleut people is a chain of volcanic islands off the Alaskan coast. These islands mark the border between the Bering Sea and the Pacific Ocean. Alaska's name comes from the Aleut word *aliasksha*, which means "land that is not an island" or "mainland." They used this term to describe the vast land to the east of their island homeland. Later, sailors traveling in the region used the name to refer to the entire area we now know as Alaska.

ALASKA

8

# READ ABOUT

Denali National
Park covers an
area larger than
the state of
Massachusetts.

CHAPTER ONE

# LAND

★

IMAGINE LIVING IN A PLACE THAT IS SO IMMENSE AND SPARSELY POPULATED THAT YOU MIGHT NOT SEE ANOTHER PERSON OUTSIDE YOUR FAMILY FOR WEEKS. Welcome to Alaska—the largest state in the country! Within its 663,267 square miles (1,717,854 square kilometers), Alaska, also known as the Last Frontier, is home to some of the world's highest mountains and most remote wilderness areas. Its highest point is Denali at 20,320 feet (6,194 meters), and its lowest point is at sea level along the Pacific Ocean.

The northern lights, known as the aurora borealis, brighten the sky near Anchorage.

## SEE IT HERE!

### LOOK UP IN THE SKY

One of the most amazing sights in Alaska is the northern lights, also known as the aurora borealis. These dancing ribbons of color light up the night sky during more than half the year. The scientific explanation does not sound nearly as exciting as the results. The energy from the sun is typically drawn to the polar regions by the earth's magnetic field. When this energy hits the gas particles in the upper atmosphere, they light up in colors. Some people say that when these lights ripple across the sky, they can feel the hair stand up on their arms and the back of their necks!

## THE LAND OF EXTREMES

One of the most impressive things about Alaska is its size. It is almost impossible to grasp how large it is, even when you look at all of the statistics. The distance from north to south, for example, is 1,700 miles (2,700 km), the same as the distance from northern Maine to the southern tip of Florida. Compared to the rest of the county, Alaska comes in first in total land and inland and coastal water areas.

Alaska's shape is unusual. On a map it looks like a large square sitting on top of two spindly, long legs, which are actually the Panhandle in the southeast and the Alaskan

Peninsula and the Aleutian Islands in the southwest. It is little surprise that **naturalist** John Muir, who saw many fascinating parts of the world during his travels, once wrote, "To the lover of pure wilderness, Alaska is one of the most wonderful countries in the world."

Not only is it the largest state in the country, it is also home to the biggest national park, the largest state park, the longest chain of volcanoes, and **glaciers** as big as some of the country's smaller states. It has the longest periods of daylight and darkness of any area in the United States.

Alaska sits north of the continental United States. Alaskans often refer to the rest of the country as the Lower 48 or the South 48. Alaska is surrounded on the north by the Arctic Ocean and on the south by the Gulf of Alaska and the Pacific Ocean. To the west are the Bering Sea, the Chukchi Sea, and Russia. Canada lies to the east.

## WORDS TO KNOW

**naturalist** *a person who studies natural history*

**glaciers** *slow-moving masses of ice*

# Alaska Geo-Facts

Along with the state's geographical highlights, this chart ranks Alaska's land, water, and total area compared to all other states.

**Total area; rank** . . . . . . . . .663,267 square miles (1,717,854 sq km); 1st
**Land; rank** . . . . . . . . . . . . .571,951 square miles (1,481,347 sq km); 1st
**Water; rank** . . . . . . . . . . . . . 91,316 square miles (236,507 sq km); 1st
**Inland water; rank** . . . . . . . . 17,243 square miles (44,659 sq km); 1st
**Coastal water; rank** . . . . . . . 27,049 square miles (70,057 sq km); 1st
**Territorial water; rank** . . . . . . . . . .47,024 square miles (121,792); 1st
**Geographic center** . . . . . . . . . . . . . . . . . . . 60 miles (97 km) northwest
    of Denali, 63° 50′ N, 152° W
**Latitude** . . . . . . . . . . . . . . . . . . . . . . . . . . 54° 40′ N to 71° 50′ N
**Longitude** . . . . . . . . . . . . . . . . . . . . . . . . . 130° W to 173° E
**Highest point** . . . . . . . . . . . . . . . . . . .Denali, 20,320 feet (6,194 m)
**Lowest point** . . . . . . . . . . . . . . . . . . . Sea level at the Pacific Ocean
**Largest city** . . . . . . . . . . . . . . . . . . . . . . . . . . . . . . . .Anchorage
**Longest river** . . . . . . . . . . . . .Yukon River, 1,875 miles (3,018 km)

Source: U.S. Census Bureau

 Alaska is so enormous, Texas could fit inside it twice, and little Rhode Island could fit 500 times!

# Alaska's Topography

Use the color-coded elevation chart to see on the map Alaska's high points (purple to red) and low points (green to dark green). Elevation is measured as the distance above or below sea level.

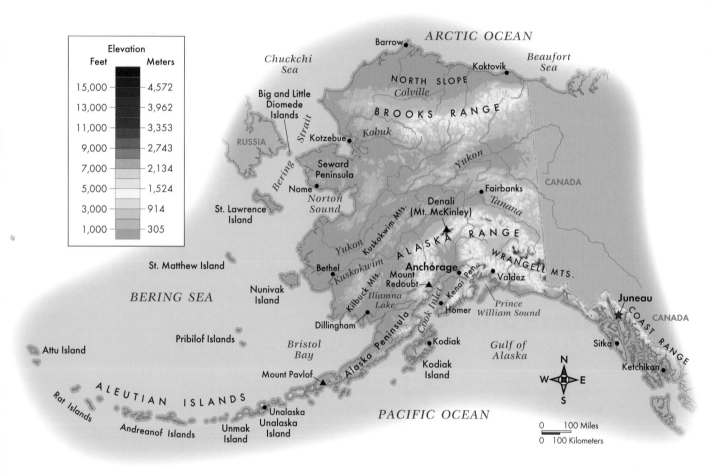

At 6,640 miles (10,686 km), the coastline of Alaska is longer than the combined coastlines of all the other states.

## LAND REGIONS

Geographically, Alaska can be described as having six main regions: the North Slope, Western Alaska, the Aleutian Region, the Interior, Southcentral Alaska, and Southeastern Alaska. Each region is unique.

An aerial view of Barrow reveals how isolated the town is.

## The North Slope

The North Slope is sometimes known as the Arctic Coastal Plain. This region is entirely within the Arctic Circle. Its largest city is Barrow. This region is commonly called the Land of the Midnight Sun. That's because as a result of the tilt of Earth, the sun rises here around May 10 and does not set until around August 2—84 days later!

Much of this region is **tundra**, and the ground is hard with **permafrost**, sometimes reaching as far down as several thousand feet. Because the top of this soil is so hard, rain cannot soak into the ground on the few occasions when it occurs. Despite this deep freeze, for a few weeks during the summer the surface ice melts and forms puddles. Suddenly, berry bushes and bright wildflowers bloom, bringing welcome color to the stark landscape.

Although this is not a very welcoming place for people, it is for many animals. Millions of migrating birds nest here for a time, while caribou and bears roam the area, enjoying the plentiful food sources. Off the coasts, whales, seals, and walruses swim in the waters.

### WORDS TO KNOW

**tundra** *treeless plains*

**permafrost** *a permanently frozen layer of soil*

## Western Alaska

The western part of this big state reaches out into the Bering Sea. This region includes Seward Peninsula and the Yukon and Kuskokwim river deltas. The Kilbuck and Kuskokwim mountain ranges tower over the land, and there are thousands of lakes—many of them so small that they do not even have names. Off the coast are several of Alaska's islands, including Nunivak Island and Little Diomede, which is only a few miles from Russia's Big Diomede Island. The cities of Nome, Bethel, and Dillingham are located in western Alaska.

There is a lot of volcanic activity in the Aleutian mountain range. Mount Pavlof is there. It has erupted more than 40 times since 1790. The biggest eruption to date, which occurred in 1911, sent so much ash into the air that it darkened the sky over much of the Northern Hemisphere. This western region also includes Kodiak Island, the second largest island in the United States after Hawaii.

Homes on the coast of Kodiak Island

## Aleutian Region

The Aleutian Region of Alaska includes the Aleutian Archipelago (an archipelago is a string of islands, usually in an arc) and the Alaska Peninsula. Together, they extend more than 1,400 miles (2,250 km) westward into the Pacific Ocean. The Aleutian Archipelago is made up of more than 150 small islands that were created by ancient volcanoes. Many of them are round and treeless with craggy shores. Unalaska is the eastern border of the chain, while the farthest island to the west is Attu Island.

## The Interior

Alaska's Interior is the largest of all its regions. Two of its borders are roughly created by mountain ranges. The Alaska Range is in the south while the Brooks Range is in the north. The Interior, or central uplands and lowlands, is full of gently rolling hills and several large rivers, including 1,265 miles (2,036 m) of the Yukon, the third longest river in the United States, and the Tanana. The tallest mountain range in all of North America soars to 20,320 feet (6,194 m) in the Alaskan Interior. Although for a time it was called Mount McKinley, in honor of U.S. president William McKinley, in 1975 it returned to its original name, Denali, an Athabascan word meaning "the great one."

## Southcentral Alaska

Just above the Gulf of Alaska is the area known as Southcentral Alaska. This is where most of the state's people live. It includes Anchorage, the biggest city in Alaska. Anchorage is more than eight times larger than Alaska's second and third biggest cities, Fairbanks and Juneau (which are roughly the same size). It also

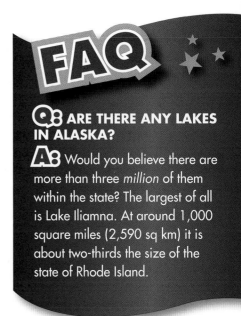

**FAQ**

**Q8 ARE THERE ANY LAKES IN ALASKA?**

**A8** Would you believe there are more than three *million* of them within the state? The largest of all is Lake Iliamna. At around 1,000 square miles (2,590 sq km) it is about two-thirds the size of the state of Rhode Island.

Hikers rest by a pool on a glacier in
Wrangell-Saint Elias National Park.

contains the Matanuska-Susitna Valleys, the Kenai
Peninsula, and the Prince William Sound shoreline.
The Wrangell–Saint Elias National Park is here. It is the
largest national park in the United States. Ten active
volcanoes can be found in this region, along with the
majority of Alaska's glaciers. Two of the biggest glaciers
in Alaska are the Malaspina and the Bering. These
glaciers cover a total of more than 2,300 square miles
(6,000 sq km). The state of Rhode Island could fit on
each one with lots of room left over!

## Southeastern Alaska

This area is known as the Panhandle. It is defined by the shape and flow of water. It is made up of a narrow strip of islands, inlets, and peninsulas, including an area known as the Inside Passage. This is a 15,000-mile (24,000 km) strip of coastline with more than 1,000 islands, coves, and bays. Many of the cities within this region can be reached only by the ferries of the Alaska Marine Highway System.

## CLIMATE

Although you might think Alaska is covered with ice and snow year-round, this is far from true. In a land as large as Alaska, the weather can change dramatically if you just travel far enough. The climate in the southern portion of the state is affected by its closeness to the sea. The ocean winds help to keep the temperatures fairly moderate, neither extremely hot nor extremely cold.

Extremes in temperature are usually found in the Interior, where it is not unusual for the temperatures to rise to over 90 degrees F (32 degrees Celsius) during the summer and plummet to –80°F (–62°C) in the winter. The Panhandle has a lot of rain but little snow. The North Slope is terribly windy, with bitterly cold gusts that send most of its snow into deep drifts. Summer, on the other hand, can be quite comfortable in Alaska. Temperatures often reach into the 55°F (13°C) range and occasionally top 60°F (16°C).

In many parts of Alaska, winter is for only the toughest of creatures. The snow can start as early as September and last well into May. Temperatures often go below 32 degrees F (0 degrees C), and because of the howling wind, they feel even lower. **Frostbite** and

## MANY WORDS FOR WIND

Alaska is very windy. Alaskans have special names for each type of wind that blows. The *chinook* is a warm wind carrying promises of spring. A *taku* is a bitterly cold arctic wind that roars across the land at speeds up to 100 miles per hour (160 kph). The *williwaws* are sudden, unexpected gusts.

## WORD TO KNOW

**frostbite** *partial freezing of parts of the body exposed to extreme cold*

# Weather Report

This chart shows record temperatures (high and low) for the state, as well as average temperatures (July and January) and average annual precipitation.

**Record high temperature** . . . . . . . . . . . . . . . . . . . . . 100°F  (38°C)
    at Fort Yukon on June 27, 1915
**Record low temperature** . . . . . . . . . . . . . . . . . . . . –80°F  (–62°C)
    at Prospect Creek, near Stevens Village, on January 23, 1971
**Average July temperature, Anchorage** . . . . . . . . . . . 58°F (14°C)
**Average January temperature, Anchorage** . . . . . . . 16°F (–9°C)
**Average July temperature, Barrow** . . . . . . . . . . . . . . 40°F (4°C)
**Average January temperature, Barrow** . . . . . . . . –14°F (–26°C)
**Average annual precipitation, Anchorage** . . . . 16 inches (41 cm)
**Average annual precipitation, Barrow** . . . . . . . 4 inches (10 cm)

Source: National Climatic Data Center, NESDIS, NOAA, U.S. Dept. of Commerce

## WORDS TO KNOW

**hypothermia** *abnormally low body temperature that threatens a person's ability to function physically and mentally*

**magnitude** *a mathematical scale to measure the strength of something*

**Richter scale** *the scale developed to measure the strength of an earthquake*

**epicenter** *the focal or main point of an earthquake*

hypothermia are common and potentially dangerous problems for those people who are not prepared properly for the cold.

### When the Earth Shakes

Each day, 50 to 100 earthquakes shake Alaska. That works out to almost 24,000 quakes a year. In fact, just over half of the earthquakes in the entire United States each year occur in Alaska. Every dozen years or so, Alaska is shaken by a quake with a **magnitude** of 8 or higher. Smaller ones, ranging between 4 and 5 on the Richter scale, happen about 90 times a year. This is because of the constant shifting of the tectonic plates under the earth's surface in this region.

Three of the largest earthquakes ever measured on the planet have occurred in Alaska. One, centered in the Andreanof Islands in 1957, had a magnitude 8.6. Another, in the Rat Islands in 1965, measured 8.7 on the **Richter scale**. The country's largest earthquake on record, with a magnitude of 9.2, occurred on March 27, 1964. Its **epicenter** was Prince William Sound. Combined, the earthquake and the resulting tsunami (tidal wave) took 131 lives and caused about $311 million in property loss (in 1964 dollars).

In addition to quakes, Alaskans also have to watch out for a different kind of rumbling—erupting volcanoes! In 1989, Mount Redoubt erupted. In 1996, Mount Pavlof erupted twice, sending ash into the sky.

## PLANT LIFE

Growing out of Alaska's cold soil are mosses and lichens, as well as willow trees that leaf out in the summertime. While a good portion of Alaska is made up of treeless plains, about one-quarter of the state is forested. Short birch and spruce trees grow in the sparse **taiga** forests. In the **boreal** forests, the trees are much thicker. During the brief summers when temperatures rise, bursts of color can be seen from flowers such as wild asters, violets, lupines, and larkspurs. Fireweed grows alongside highways, and more than 500 types of wild mushrooms grow in the forests. Blueberries, cranberries, and strawberries, as well as the more exotic lingonberries, crowberries, and soapberries, all grow in Alaska.

## ANIMAL LIFE

Although relatively few humans live in Alaska, it is home to plenty of living creatures. Such animals as wolves,

Smoke and ash rise from the Augustine Volcano on Augustine Island in 2006.

### WORDS TO KNOW

**taiga** *forests that are found in cold, wet climates only*

**boreal** *of or belonging to the north*

Lingonberries and red leaves of the alpine bearberry peek out from among lichen.

A humpback whale leaps from the water in Frederick Sound in southeastern Alaska.

## WORD TO KNOW

**pesticide** *any chemical or biological agent used to kill plant or animal pests*

mountain goats, moose, and hundreds of thousands of caribou can be found there. Musk oxen were once a common sight but by the mid-1800s they had been hunted to extinction in the area. Later, conservationists brought oxen from Greenland to Alaska and started a new population of them. Bears are a common sight in Alaska. There are black bears in the southern and

## ENDANGERED SPECIES

Although there are a lot of species of animals and plants living in Alaska, some of them are not thriving. The short-tailed albatross and the Eskimo curlew are two birds that are endangered in Alaska. Also endangered are the leatherback sea turtle, the eastern Steller sea lions, and three types of whales: the bowhead, finback, and humpback. Alaskan species that are considered threatened are the northern sea otter, the western Steller sea lion, and ducklike birds known as the Steller's eider and the spectacled eider.

Thanks to the help of wildlife biologists, the Arctic peregrine falcon has been brought back from the brink of extinction and even taken off the endangered list. As a result of the use of a **pesticide** known as DDT in the 1970s, these birds laid eggs with shells too thin to protect the young inside. The bird population plummeted. DDT was banned in the United States. Biologists in Alaska raised some falcons in captivity, taught them how to hunt, and then released them into the wild. By 1994, the falcons were no longer considered endangered.

interior regions, polar bears searching for seals on the coasts, and huge, brown, grizzly bears of the Kodiak. When grizzly bears stand up, they often are more than 10 feet (3 m) tall!

The waters surrounding Alaska contain 15 different species of whales, as well as fur seals, walruses, and five species of salmon. In fact, the schools of wild salmon swimming in Alaska's waters are the largest of anywhere in the world.

Alaska's skies are full of more than 400 species of birds. Some live in Alaska

## GEORG WILHELM STELLER: EXPLORER AND MORE

Although Georg Wilhelm Steller (1709–1746) did not reach Alaska until 1741, he clearly led an exotic life before then. Born in Germany, his life's work was studying the plants and animals of different regions. He explored Russia extensively and then went to Alaska as part of Vitus Bering's expedition. He wrote about many of the new species he observed there. A number of the state's plants and animals are named after him, including Steller's jay, Steller's sea lion, and Steller's eider.

Want to know more? See www.acsu.buffalo.edu/~insrisg/nature/nw99/steller.html

A grizzly bear about to catch a salmon in Katmai National Park

Tufted puffins on
St. Paul Island

year-round, while others pass through once a year to visit and nest. One, the arctic tern, continues to astound scientists with its ability to fly 22,000 miles (35,400 km) round trip during its annual migration from Alaska to Antarctica. Other feathered Alaska residents include bald eagles, snow owls, puffins, and ravens. Lakes and marshes are home to millions of ducks, trumpeter swans, and Canada and snow geese.

## THE HEAT IS ON!

Global warming is an issue that concerns people all over the world. In Alaska, it is an especially serious matter. Over the last century, temperatures there have increased twice as much as they have in the rest of the world, gaining 3 to 5°F (1 to 3°C). How do a few degrees make a difference? According to some experts, even a small change in temperature can have dramatic results. For example, Alaska's typical cold weather prevents nonnative

### MINI-BIO

## ADA BLACKJACK: ARCTIC SURVIVOR

Born in Solomon, Alaska, Ada Blackjack (1898–1983) was a strong woman. At age 23, she joined a Russian expedition as the cook and seamstress. In September 1921, she and four men were stranded on Wrangell Island, north of Siberia. They were there for months. They ran out of food and three of the men left to find help. They never returned. The fourth man died, leaving Ada totally alone for several months. She lived by hunting ducks, seals, and white foxes, which she cooked into stews and broths. By the time she was finally rescued on August 23, 1923, she was living on little more than tea and hard biscuits.

**?** **Want to know more?** See *Ada Blackjack: A True Story of Survival in the Arctic* by Jennifer Niven (Hyperion, 2003).

plants, or invasive species, from spreading and pushing out the native plants. Warmer temperatures mean the invasive plants will grow more abundantly and threaten native species. The warmer temperatures also melt the glaciers, sending extra water into the oceans which may eventually raise the sea level.

In July 2005, the track from a three-toed dinosaur estimated to be 70 million years old was found in Denali National Park. It was the first evidence that these animals had been in the region.

# Alaska National Park Areas

This map shows some of Alaska's national parks, monuments, preserves, and other areas protected by the National Park Service.

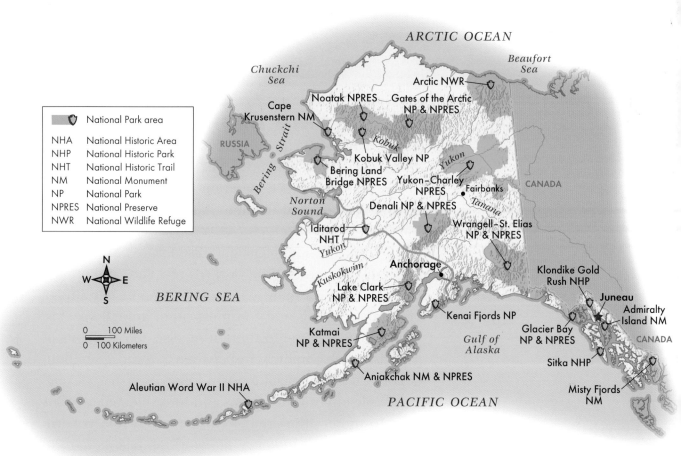

A herd of caribou crosses a river in the Arctic National Wildlife Refuge.

## AN ONGOING ARGUMENT

There has been much discussion and controversy about a small Alaskan town called Kaktovik. Many of its nearly 300 residents depend on hunting, whaling, and fishing for food and income. Kaktovik is in the Arctic National Wildlife Refuge (ANWR), which was created in 1960 by President Dwight Eisenhower and placed under federal protection, or the direct care and protection of the government. This refuge is home to millions of migratory birds and countless other animal species. The ANWR is home to something else, too—billions of gallons of oil, somewhere between 5.7 and 16 billion, depending on what source you follow.

While environmentalists and some elected officials fight to protect the area, some people in the government and the oil industry are working just as hard to find a way to drill for that oil. Environmentalists worry that pipelines and drilling—and possible oil spills—threaten wildlife and the environment. Those people in favor of drilling claim that the drilling will have limited environmental impact because only 8 percent of the refuge would be affected. In addition, they claim that the billions of gallons of domestic oil will decrease the country's dependence on foreign oil, bring money to Alaska, and provide much-needed jobs. Because the land is under federal protection, both Congress and the president must grant permission to open it to exploration and drilling.

What do Alaskans think? Some are in favor—they want the jobs and the increased revenue for their home state. Others are not so sure.

**THINK ABOUT IT!**

# Drilling in ANWR?

## PRO

Many people believe that drilling for oil in ANWR will provide jobs and benefit the country. Alaska senator Ted Stevens says, "I think it is in the national interest to be able to produce from ANWR, and certainly, by the time we could get it ready to produce it would be a ready reserve."

## CON

Other people believe that drilling in ANWR is not a solution. Athan Manuel, the Sierra Club's lands protection program director, says, "It's time for drilling-obsessed politicians to stop stalling with bad ideas. America needs new policies that invest in our energy future, not more favors for the very industry that is keeping us oil addicted."

## READ ABOUT

This is how the Bering Land Bridge National Preserve looks today. Thousands of years ago, people crossed this land and settled in what is now Alaska.

**40,000 years ago**

*Asia and North America are connected by a narrow piece of land*

◄ **30,000–10,000 years ago**

*People begin crossing from Asia into what is now Alaska*

**6,000–9,000 years ago**

*A group of people comes from northeast Siberia*

C H A P T E R   T W O

# FIRST PEOPLE

★

A LASKA'S HERITAGE IS RICH. More than 40,000 years ago, the sea level was lower and the land between Asia and North America became exposed. Many historians believe that this allowed people to move from one area of the world to another, including from Asia into what would one day become Alaska.

**3000 BCE**
*People begin moving into northern Alaska*

**900 to 1300 CE**
*People continue migrating into Alaska*

▲ **8,400 years ago**
*People are living on the Aleutian Islands*

Paleo-Indians migrated across the Bering land bridge and hunted seals, elk, and other animals.

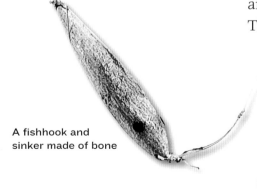

A fishhook and sinker made of bone

## PREHISTORIC ALASKA

The first people to live in what is now Alaska were Paleo-Indians, who probably walked to the region from Asia. They hunted seals, fish, and whales in the water, as well as elk, bears, caribou, and mammoths on land. Berries and nuts were harvested whenever they could be found. These early people made use of almost all parts of the animals they hunted. The meat was eaten immediately or preserved by being dried or smoked. The fat was used for cooking, put into oil lamps, or used for waterproofing clothing and boats. Bones were made into

# Native Alaskan Peoples

## (Before European Contact)

This map shows the general area of Native Alaskan people before European settlers arrived.

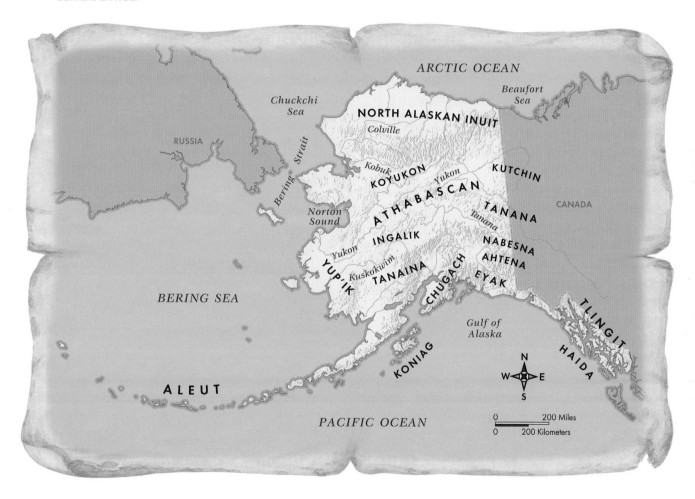

everything imaginable, from eating utensils and fish-hooks to needles and tools. Skins were made into clothing and shoes, as well as lining for the walls and floors of homes and the interiors of boats. Little was wasted.

Some people traveled the icy and snowy terrain by dogsled. They made the sleds out of driftwood and

## SEE IT HERE!

### ANANIULIAK ISLAND

At the Anangula site on Ananiuliak Island, **archaeologists** have discovered ancient stones and blade tools that are believed to date to the earliest known human settlement in the Aleutians—about 8,400 years ago. At the site are the remains of a village once occupied by Eskimo-Aleuts. There you can see evidence of underground houses and remains of workshops outside the houses.

## WORD TO KNOW

**archaeologists** *people who study the remains of past human societies*

animal bones lashed together with animal skins. The dog harnesses were commonly made from caribou hides. This method of travel is still used in parts of Alaska today.

In the beginning, the people who journeyed to this part of the world were very similar. As they began to move into different areas of what would become Alaska, they separated into groups that developed their own languages, cultures, and ways of life.

## ATHABASCANS

Athabascan people migrated to the interior of Alaska, to an area extending from the Brooks Range south to the Kenai Peninsula. They lived along waterways, moving whenever the fish and game moved with the seasons. Their way of life focused on sharing resources, a custom that continues with those Athabascans who still live in Alaska today.

For centuries, people in Alaska have traveled by dogsled.

Athabascans lived in groups of 20 to 40 people. Although they had a few established base camps, they spent most of their time moving from one place to another as food sources changed. Their clothing and moccasins were made out of animal hides, and both the men and women of this group knew how to sew well. Depending heavily on trade, they used birchbark canoes to visit other communities, as well as dogsleds and sturdy snowshoes.

## YUP'IKS AND CUP'IKS

Settling into the southwestern portion of the state, these Alaska Natives were named for the two primary languages they speak. Like the Athabascans, these peoples moved frequently, traveling from one place to another, following animals' migration patterns.

Men and women lived separately. The men stayed in a *qasgiq*, where they learned how to hunt, while women lived in an *ena*, where they learned to cook using a fan-shaped knife called an *uluaq*, and to sew using needles made of stone, bone, and walrus ivory. Clothing was typically made from animal skins and sometimes waterproofed with fish skin or marine mammal intestines. Grass was added to socks to make them thicker and warmer.

## INUPIAQS

The word *Inupiaq* means "real people." When these people arrived from across the Bering Strait, they spread out into the northern and northwestern regions of Alaska. Their lifestyle centered on being near water where they could find whale, walrus, seal, and fish. They were known for their use of flint and gouging tools. Some of them branched off to live on Kodiak Island and the upper Alaska Peninsula.

A group of Inupiaqs travel through Grantley Harbor at the beginning of the 20th century.

Inupiaqs made their homes, or *barabaras*, out of pieces of grassy earth called sod. Often the homes had an underground tunnel entrance, which was designed to trap cold air, keeping the interior warmer. The barabaras were built partly underground. The sod was placed on a frame made of whale bones, which was frequently in a dome shape.

Like many other people at the time, Inupiaqs were hunter-gatherers, living on a combination of berries and fruits found in the forest, salmon and other sea creatures from the oceans, and moose, caribou, and bison from across the land. Birds and eggs were another part of their diet. Inupiaqs traveled in boats called *umiaks* made from walrus skins stretched over a frame of driftwood. They used them to hunt and to travel to other groups for trading.

## ALEUTS

The smallest of the Alaska Native groups, the Aleuts, migrated to the end of the Alaska Peninsula and the Alaskan Islands. Most of their villages were close to the water's edge to take advantage of the plentiful fish there. They also relied on the water to travel from one spot to another.

Aleuts made needles from the bones of seagulls and used them to decorate their clothing with brightly colored threads and beads. Some of their homes were large—so large, that up to 40 families could live in one of them. Homes were built partially underground so that they would be protected from wind and cold temperatures. The entrance was through a ladder in the ceiling.

To hunt, men traveled in skin-covered canoes they called *baidarkas*. They placed seal skins on the inside to make them waterproof. They journeyed hundreds of miles in search of food for their people. In the canoes, the men wore special wooden sun hats to protect their eyes from the water's glare. It meant the man was a successful hunter if he had sea lion whiskers attached to the visor. From their canoes, the men would use nets and traps made in their village, as well as wooden hooks and lines made of seaweed, to catch larger amounts of fish.

*Picture Yourself . . .*

### Building a Umiak

The day dawns and you are already awake. You join your brothers at the edge of the sea. Yesterday, the three of you cut a driftwood log into four pieces. These will be used to make the frame of your boat. While others keep cutting wood that will become the boat's ribs, you sew the seal skins together with **sinew**. This will take the rest of the day, but you know that within a few days you will be able to stretch these skins over the wooden framework the others are putting together. Right now, the umiak is just a pile of wood and skins, but soon it will become the boat that will take you on journeys you can only dream about today.

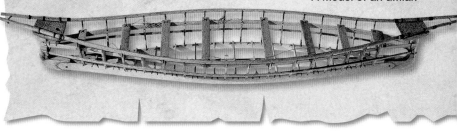

A model of an umiak

### WORD TO KNOW

**sinew** *an inflexible cord or band of connective tissue that joins muscle to bone*

## BLUE BABE

In 1979, a fossil of a long-horned bison was found near Fairbanks. A gold miner was digging and saw hooves, hide, and flesh. Because of the soil's minerals, the bison looked blue. Examination showed "Blue Babe" was 35 centuries old, had been killed by lions, fell into a river, froze, and was buried.

Want to know more? See www.alaska.edu/opa/eInfo/index.xml?StoryID=180

## EYAKS, TLINGITS, HAIDAS, AND TSIMSHIANS

Although Eyaks, Tlingits, Haidas, and Tsimshians are all related, they spoke different languages. Eyaks occupied the southeastern corner of south-central Alaska, while Tlingits lived mainly in the southeast panhandle of Alaska. Haidas and Tsimshians settled on the islands in southeastern Alaska: Haidas preferred the Prince of Wales Island area, and Tsimshians lived on Annette Island.

The different groups built homes that were as large as 100 feet by 75 feet (30 m by 23 m), each with cedar

This engraving by artist Paolo Fumagalli depicts a Native village in Alaska.

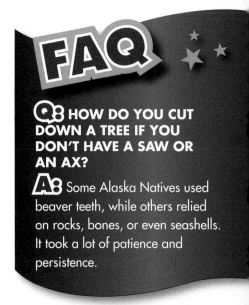

bark or spruce shingles on the roof. Each home had a central fire pit and could hold between 20 and 50 people at a time.

Winter villages were set up along waterways so that the people could easily access food and drinking water. Along with these winter bases, the groups had seasonal camps that they moved to and from when following animal migration patterns or harvests. Fish of all kinds were caught, and salmon was a popular dish.

Because south-central and southeastern Alaska had many trees, wood was important to these peoples. Everything from houses and daily utensils to boats and clothing was made from wood or its products.

A fire was often in the center of an Alaskan Indian home.

## FAQ ★ ★ ★

**Q8 HOW DO YOU CUT DOWN A TREE IF YOU DON'T HAVE A SAW OR AN AX?**

**A8** Some Alaska Natives used beaver teeth, while others relied on rocks, bones, or even seashells. It took a lot of patience and persistence.

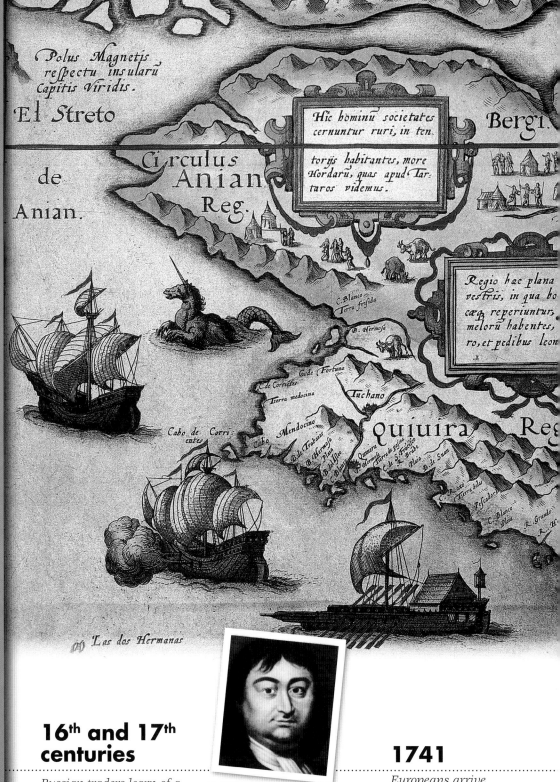

**READ ABOUT**

A map from 1593 notes the Bering Strait (El Streto de Anian).

## 16th and 17th centuries

*Russian traders learn of a "Great Land" somewhere to the east*

## 1728 ▲

*Vitus Bering sails through what becomes known as the Bering Strait*

## 1741

*Europeans arrive in Alaska*

# CHAPTER THREE

# EXPLORATION AND SETTLEMENT

★

ALTHOUGH ALASKA HAS VAST LAND AND RESOURCES, IT TOOK A LONG TIME FOR MOST OF THE WORLD TO FIND IT. In the late 16th century, Europeans became aware of this region, but it was another two centuries before they began to seriously explore this large frontier. By the time the Europeans arrived, Native people had inhabited Alaska for thousands of years.

**1774**
*Juan Pérez lands on what is now Prince of Wales Island*

**1778 ▶**
*James Cook explores the Alaska area for Great Britain*

**1784**
*The first Russian colony in North America is established at Three Saints Bay (now Kodiak)*

## THE ARRIVAL OF THE EUROPEANS

The first non-Native people to come to Alaska were from Russia. For hundreds of years, Russian fur hunters and traders in Siberia had heard stories from sailors, traders, and explorers of a great land beyond the sea to the east. In 1728, Peter the Great, tsar, or ruler, of Russia, appointed Vitus Bering, a Danish officer in the Russian navy, to investigate this mysterious land.

Bering's first trip was not a success. Unknown to him, he neared the Alaskan coast (on what would later be called the Bering Strait), but storms and ice stopped him from seeing the shore, and he never landed. Not

Vitus Bering's 1741 expedition visited some of the Aleutian Islands before his ship the *St. Peter* wrecked.

about to give up, Bering made another journey in 1741. This time, he and his two ships, the *St. Paul* and the *St. Peter*, reached Alaska. But the two ships became separated. In July, the *St. Paul* reached land at Noyes Island or Jacobi Island. The next day, the *St. Peter* reached land at Kayak Island. Months later, the *St. Peter* ran aground near the island now known as Bering Island in the Aleutians, and it was destroyed. Stuck on the island and sick with **scurvy**, Bering and some of his crew died. The survivors eventually built a boat from the wreckage of the *St. Peter* and set sail for home. Meanwhile, the *St. Paul* had returned to Siberia. The crews' cargoes of fox, fur seal, and sea otter pelts, and their stories of what they had seen, made others want to return to this great land.

## VITUS BERING: DANISH EXPLORER

Vitus Jonassen Bering (1681–1741) was born in Denmark. As a teenager, he became a seaman. He spent most of his life exploring new lands. Working for Russia, he led the First Kamchatka Expedition. His party traveled over 6,000 miles (10,000 km) of wilderness, trying to discover how far the Siberian mainland reached. Bad weather eventually forced him to turn back. A second mission, the Great Northern Expedition, was a terrible trip, doomed almost from the beginning. Bering got lost and then got sick. Finally, his ship ran aground near what became Bering Island and he, along with 28 members of his crew, died from scurvy.

❓ **Want to know more?** See www.pmel.noaa.gov/np/pages/vbering.html

By 1745, hunting and trading ships regularly made the trip from Siberia to Alaska. The hunters and traders searched for sea otter pelts, which were popular in Russia for hats and clothing. In fact, these pelts were so popular throughout Europe that by the end of the 1700s, the animal was almost extinct. Some of the Russian hunters had only a rough idea of how to hunt a sea otter. So, they bribed local Aleuts to help them. When bribery did not work, they kidnapped Aleuts and forced them to trap.

## WORD TO KNOW

**scurvy** *a disease resulting from a lack of vitamin C in the diet*

# European Exploration of Alaska

The colored arrows on this map show the routes taken by European explorers between 1728 and 1778.

Vitus Bering, 1728
Vitus Bering, 1741
James Cook, 1778
Early Russian settlement
Present-day state of Alaska

RUSSIA

Kamchatka Peninsula

Bering Island

Attu Island

ALEUTIAN ISLANDS

BERING SEA

St. Matthew Island

Pribilof Islands

Nunivak Island

St. Lawrence Island

Wrangell Island

Chuckchi Sea

ARCTIC OCEAN

Beaufort Sea

Colville

Yukon

Kuskokwim

Tanana

Great Bear Lake

Mackenzie

CANADA

Mt. St. Elias

New Archangel (Sitka)

Gulf of Alaska

PACIFIC OCEAN

0   200 Miles
0   200 Kilometers

N
W   E
S

## FURTHER EXPLORATION

In the 1770s, other countries took an interest in Alaska. Great Britain, Spain, and France sought ways to exploit its resources. Spain sent more than a half dozen expeditions to Alaska. In 1774, Juan Pérez landed on what is now Prince of Wales Island in Dixon Sound. Then, in 1778, England sent Captain James Cook to report on Alaska. His maps were used by sailors for the next hundred years. Over the next decade, Russia, Britain, Spain, and France fought for official ownership of the land. When the fighting was over, Russia ended up with the claim.

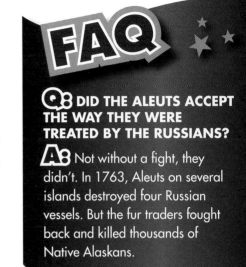

## FAQ

**Q8 DID THE ALEUTS ACCEPT THE WAY THEY WERE TREATED BY THE RUSSIANS?**

**A8** Not without a fight, they didn't. In 1763, Aleuts on several islands destroyed four Russian vessels. But the fur traders fought back and killed thousands of Native Alaskans.

This is an illustration of Alaska during Captain James Cook's 1778 expedition.

## MINI-BIO

### JAMES COOK: EXPLORER

From a young age, James Cook (1728–1779) was at home on the water. Growing up in England, he learned how to sail small ships known as colliers, which carried cargoes of coal, and then served in the British Royal Navy. In 1768, he was appointed commander of the Endeavour. In 1769, on his first expedition, he helped map New Zealand and Australia. Nine years later, he helped map Alaska. Cook was killed in 1779 during a battle in Hawaii.

**? Want to know more?** See www.mariner.org/educationalad/ageofex/cook.php

## THE NATIVE PEOPLE FIGHT BACK

By the early 1780s, Alaska was under Russian control. In 1784, the first Russian colony was established at Three Saints Bay (later Kodiak Island). Native people were not happy about this intrusion. When Russian merchant Grigorii Shelikhov sent three ships to Kodiak Island for yet more furs, he claimed the Native peoples refused to help. According to Shelikhov's account, the Native people told the

The Russians established their first Alaskan settlement on what is now Kodiak Island.

These women are sitting in front of the Sitka Trading Company. For many years, Sitka was a major fur-trading post.

Russians to get back on board and leave. Negotiations failed. Then the Russians used their cannons to destroy the people's homes. The violence did not end there. Shelikhov was so cruel to the Alaskans that the Russian government investigated his methods, but he was never officially charged with any crime.

Although the original people of Alaska fought back, Alaska was slipping out of their hands. Russians had discovered the land's vast resources, and soon other countries became aware of them, too. The demand for furs throughout Europe kept adventurers coming, and trade companies, such as the Russian-American Company, were established to meet the demand. Within the next century, another resource was discovered that would attract even more eager visitors: gold!

## ALASKA'S OLDEST SHIPWRECK

In 2003, divers found the wreck of a ship called the *Kad'yak*. The 132-foot (40 m) vessel lay 80 feet (24 m) below the surface, just off Kodiak Island. Evidence shows that it sank around 1860. One of the few items found was a brass object, believed to be the hub of the ship's wheel, with the ship's name on it.

44

An Aleut hunter paddles on the Bering Sea.

## 1802

*The Tlingit people rebel against the Russians*

## 1867

*Russia sells Alaska to the United States*

## 1898 ▶

*Thousands search for Alaskan gold*

# CHAPTER FOUR

# GROWTH AND CHANGE

★

AT THE START OF THE 19TH CENTURY, RUSSIANS STILL CONTROLLED ALASKA. The Russian-American Company, a trading company cofounded by Grigorii Shelikhov, had established fur trading posts. Alaskans were angry about losing their land and their ways of life to strangers.

▲ **1899**
*Railroad tycoon Edward Harriman leads an expedition to Alaska*

**1900**
*The state capital moves from Sitka to Juneau*

**1914** ▶
*U.S. Congress authorizes the building of an Alaskan railroad*

## MINI-BIO

### ALEXANDR BARANOV: "LORD OF ALASKA"

Russian Alexandr Baranov (1746–1819) ran away from home as a teenager. He went to Siberia and then, like other young men, was lured to Russian Alaska as a fur trader. For 19 years, he was chief manager of the Russian-American Company. As the first governor of Russian Alaska, he helped establish schools and communities throughout Alaska. At age 73, Baranov left Alaska to return to Russia, but he died on the way.

**?** **Want to know more?** See www.loc.gov/exhibits/russian/russch2.html

## INTO A NEW CENTURY

The Tlingit people were unhappy about the Russians being in their areas of Alaska. In 1802, they staged a rebellion, attacking Russian posts and killing as many Russians as they could. Their victory was short-lived. Alexandr Baranov, a fur trader hired by Shelikhov to take over the Alaskan fur business, brought a Russian warship to the area and it destroyed a Tlingit village. Baranov then rebuilt it as New Archangel (now Sitka), the capital of Russian America.

**The harbor of New Archangel as it appeared in the early 1800s**

British traders joined Alaska's fur-trading industry. Their Hudson's Bay Company had a post in Fort Yukon.

## THE MONOPOLY ENDS

Although Russia controlled Alaska and its fur trade, this began to change. The British formed the Hudson's Bay Company in 1821 and started challenging Russia's business in Alaska. Russian profits were further reduced when American hunters and trappers came to gather pelts and sell them to markets closed to the Russians. As of 1812, the Russians claimed rights to all the fur trade above **latitude** 51 degrees north, but it wasn't until 1818 that they attempted to make this claim official. At that time, Britain and the United States claimed all land below the north shore of a body of water known as the Dixon Entrance near Latitude 54 degrees north. In 1824 and 1825, this border at the Dixon Entrance was agreed upon in treaties between Russia and Great Britain as well as Russia and the United States.

## WORD TO KNOW

**latitude** *the position of a place, measured in degrees north or south of the equator*

## MINI-BIO

# IVAN VENIAMINOV: RUSSIAN MISSIONARY

Ivan Veniaminov (1797–1879) was born in Russia. At 10 years of age, he entered a seminary, a school for training ministers or priests. By 24, he was a priest, and he volunteered to go to the Aleutian Islands. There, he built a church and paddled from island to island to learn the Native languages, as well as teach the people about Christianity. Then, he created an alphabet and used it to translate religious material.

 **Want to know more?** See www.uh.edu/engines/epi668.htm

## WORD TO KNOW

**missionaries** *people who try to convert others to a religion*

As Russian interests faded in the region, some Alaska Natives, including Aleuts and Tlingits, were able to return to some of their own ways of life. However, as **missionaries** began to arrive, they brought dramatic changes.

## THE WORK OF THE MISSIONARIES

Russian Orthodox missionaries came to Alaska to run its schools and churches. Many fought to end mistreatment of the Alaskans and to protect them. Missionaries respected many of the Alaskans' cultural traditions and tried to use them in their religious teachings. Father Ivan Veniaminov helped introduce an alphabet, writing, and reading to the Native people. Today, there are nearly 90 Russian Orthodox parishes in Alaska, evidence of the early missionaries' work.

Missionaries in Alaska built many churches, such as St. Michael's Russian Orthodox Church in what is now Sitka.

## A NEW OWNER

In 1867, Russia finally agreed to give up ownership of Alaska. The Alaskan fur trade was dwindling. Both the United States and Great Britain wanted the land, and Russia preferred the United States, so it made arrangements to sell it. U.S. secretary of state William Seward, in charge of the deal, wanted Alaska's vast minerals, fish, and timber. Once again, Alaskans were not consulted. Seward bought the entire territory for $7.2 million—or about two cents per acre. On October 18, the first U.S. flag flew over Alaska.

At first, the country did not give Alaska much thought. The Civil War had just ended, and there were more pressing needs. There was no money or time to spend on this recent purchase, so Alaska was not developed for decades.

## PATROLLING THE WATERS

A key figure in U.S. history in Alaska was Captain Michael A. Healy, the first African American granted a command in what would become the U.S. Coast Guard. One of ten children born in Macon, Georgia, to an Irish immigrant and an enslaved person, Healy habitually ran away from school. His brother thought sea life would discipline the youngster, so in 1855 the 15-year-old Healy was hired as a cabin boy aboard the clipper *Jumna*. He was accepted by the Revenue Cutter Service (later part of the coast guard) in March 1865, and promoted to second lieutenant in June 1886.

Front Street in Nome in 1900, with the U.S. flag flying

**FAQ**

**Q8 WHAT DID AMERICANS THINK OF SEWARD'S PURCHASE OF ALASKA?**

**A8** Many people thought the Alaska purchase was such a mistake that they scoffed at it, calling it "Seward's Folly" and "Seward's Icebox."

Captain Michael Healy (center) on the
deck of the *Bear*

From 1887 to 1895, Healy, along with a mulitracial crew, commanded *Bear*, a ship in the Revenue Cutter Service. This service was a maritime law enforcement agency and the predecessor of the U.S. Coast Guard. The *Bear* was considered the greatest polar ship of its time, and it was charged with "seizing any vessel found sealing in the Bering Sea." By 1892, the cutters *Bear*, *Rush*, and *Corwin* had made so many seizures that tension developed between the United States and British merchants.

Promoted to first lieutenant, Healy, aboard the *Rush*, patrolled Alaskan waters. He became known as a brilliant seaman, and many considered him the best sailor in the North. A feature article in the January 28, 1884, *New York Sun* stated: "Captain Mike Healy is a good deal more distinguished person in the waters of the far Northwest than any president of the United States or any potentate in Europe has yet become."

Healy also brought medical and other aid to Alaska's Native people, made weather and ice reports, prepared navigation charts, rescued distressed vessels, transported special passengers and supplies, and fought those who violated federal laws. For many years, Healy served as a deputy U.S. marshal and represented federal law in Alaska. Between 1871 and 1888, he is credited with saving the lives of 400 seamen from whaling ships lost in the Arctic Ocean.

On one of *Bear*'s annual visits to King Island, Healy found a Native population that was down to 100 survivors who were facing starvation. After ordering food and clothing, Healy worked with Dr. Sheldon Jackson of the Bureau of Education to bring reindeer from the Siberian Chukchi, another Native group. During the next ten years, U.S. revenue cutters brought 1,100 reindeer to Alaska. The Bureau of Education took charge

Captain Healy helped bring large numbers of reindeer to King Island.

of landing and distributing the deer, and missionary schools taught the Native Alaskans how to raise and care for them. By 1940, Alaska's domesticated reindeer herds had risen to 500,000. In acknowledgment of his inspiring work, including his invaluable assistance to Alaska Natives, the U.S. Coast Guard named an ice-breaker for Michael Healy.

## VENTURING INTO A NEW LAND

Although many Americans ignored Alaska, natural-ists were excited by it. Scientists wanted to explore and study previously unknown species of plants and animals in the frozen North. A number of expeditions were organized.

From 1859 to 1863, Robert Kennicott led an expedi-tion to the Yukon for the Smithsonian Institution. He sent 40 boxes of samples back to Washington, D.C. In 1897, the Jessup Expedition, sponsored by the American Museum of Natural History, explored the life, lan-guages, and cultures of Alaska's Native populations.

In 1899, another expedition to Alaska was led by rail-road tycoon Edward Harriman. He, along with scientists and artists, surveyed the Alaskan coast for two months. Although he definitely went to make a profit, he also loved the outdoors. Harriman returned with more than 100 trunks of specimens, plus 5,000 photos and illustrations. Scientists published 13 vol-umes of his data. In 2001, 19 scientists, writers, and artists retraced Harriman's voyage, following his route and keep-ing track of changes that had occurred since his journeys.

## THE HARRIMAN EXPEDITION

The following poem was written to describe the 1899 expedition:

Bug hunters, mole catchers and trappers of mice,
Diggers of worms and experts on ice,
Pickers of posies and pounders of rock,
Bird whistlers and skinners, quite a flock
Some to hunt monsters and weeds of the sea
And there was one at least who could climb up a tree.

# GOLD!

In the last decades of the 19th century, a new type of Alaskan resource was discovered. Gold was found in 1861 in the Stikine River and in 1872 near Sitka. Four years later, it was found south of Juneau. In 1880, Joseph Juneau, Richard Harris, and their three Tlingit guides found gold elsewhere in southeastern Alaska. Finally, in 1896 the cry of "Gold!" could be heard across the country. Suddenly, the huge land that had been ignored had everyone's attention. People flocked to the area, and towns sprang up wherever gold was found. Tents turned into cities overnight. With gold miners came businesspeople who made fortunes by selling clothing, tents, food, and tools to miners.

A prospector in Alaska around 1898 searches for gold.

Searching for gold was an adventure but was rarely successful and was often difficult. In winter months, people struggled against the freezing temperatures, and in summer they contended with clouds of flies and mosquitoes. Occasionally, one person would claim a plot of land that already belonged to someone else—known as claim jumping—and violence would break out.

## "NINETY-EIGHTERS"

In 1898, Nome was founded when gold was discovered there. Tens of thousands of "ninety-eighters" rushed to Nome from the Klondike gold fields. Adventurers of all ethnic backgrounds filled the streets. Melvin Dempsey, of

Gold miners gather supplies and then get in line to climb a pass during the 1898 gold rush.

## SEE IT HERE!

### KLONDIKE GOLD RUSH NATIONAL MUSEUM

Stop by Skagway and see the Klondike Gold Rush National Museum. Take a guided tour along the 33-mile (53 km) Chilkoot Trail to follow the path both gold seekers and Native Alaskans took long ago. Here, Tlingit people walked to other areas to trade seal oil, hides, and fish with other groups. Later, gold miners tramped along in search of the best place to pan for gold.

African and Cherokee descent, arrived in the new town of Valdez in 1898. He became a gold prospector and merchant, and he opened a relief station on the Valdez Glacier. He reportedly opened Alaska's first reading room. He also became the postmaster of his mining camp on the Chistochina River, a site that now bears his name.

The United States stationed the black 24th Infantry in Alaska to keep order during the gold rush. The infantrymen were stationed at the start of the 20-mile (32 km) climb at remote Chilkoot Pass. May Mason, a black resident of Seattle, Washington, was one of several daring women who sought fortune in Alaska during the 1898 gold rush. She returned home with $5,000 in gold dust. When she was married, a Seattle paper reported that "her ears and fingers sparkled with diamonds." Other men and women prospectors were not that lucky.

Mattie Crosby, another African American, came to Alaska in 1900 with a Maine family who had adopted her and 26 other children. She was successful at business and known as a fabulous cook.

As cities formed, Alaska required regular mail delivery, schools, and supplies. Steamboats occasionally arrived with vital supplies but not during months when the rivers froze. Schools often had no textbooks or paper, and teachers had to rely on little more than

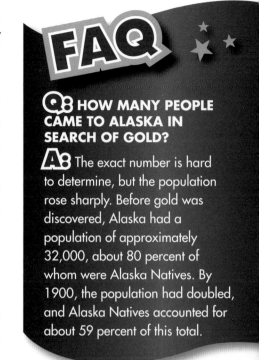

**FAQ**

**Q8 HOW MANY PEOPLE CAME TO ALASKA IN SEARCH OF GOLD?**

**A8** The exact number is hard to determine, but the population rose sharply. Before gold was discovered, Alaska had a population of approximately 32,000, about 80 percent of whom were Alaska Natives. By 1900, the population had doubled, and Alaska Natives accounted for about 59 percent of this total.

African American soldiers stand at attention in Skagway, around 1900.

the Bible and scraps of paper for their classes. When a contractor tried to use horses to deliver the mail, the first trip killed almost a dozen horses, cost $3,000, and only delivered three letters. Finally, mail carriers began to use dogsleds, and at last, letters could arrive in this vast land. One man wrote in 1897, "To see the excitement that the mail from outside makes . . . the trembling hands as they are opened, and the filling eyes as they read, touches the heart."

Like other schools, this public school in Valdez relied on supplies brought in by steamboats and dogsleds.

## THE TURN OF THE CENTURY

Workers reconstruct a railroad bridge in south-central Alaska in 1919.

In 1900, Juneau became the capital of Alaska. Twelve years later, Congress declared Alaska an official U.S. territory. As more and more people began to pour into the area, transportation became a bigger problem. By 1907, more than 230 ships had brought thousands of people to western Alaska. In 1914, plans were made to start an Alaskan railroad. The idea was to connect the Alaskan harbors on the southern coast to the mine and coal fields in the interior and to the gold claims. As the railroad was being built, several thousand workers' tents surrounded the area, which eventually became Anchorage. The first train traveled from Seward to Anchorage in 1918, signaling that the southern half of the track was done. The train system was finished in 1923. As the 20th century began, Alaska Territory was booming.

A car motors down the Alcan Highway in 1948.

**1942**
*Japan invades the
Aleutian Islands*

▲**1959**
*Alaska becomes the
49th state*

**1964**
*The Good Friday
earthquake strikes*

# CHAPTER FIVE

# MORE MODERN TIMES

★

IN THE 20TH CENTURY, AMERICANS LEARNED THAT THE PURCHASE OF ALASKA HAD NOT BEEN A FOLLY BUT A WISE DECISION. Alaska was a valuable addition to the country. The movement toward statehood slowly continued. Today, Alaska still brims with adventure and excitement as the Last Frontier.

▲ **1977**
*The Trans-Alaska pipeline is completed*

**1989** ▲
*The Exxon Valdez spills oil in Prince William Sound*

**2001**
*The governor issues the Millennium Agreement, pledging to consult with Native Alaskans*

## WORLD WAR II

Being far from the rest of the United States has had some advantages for Alaska. For example, while the rest of the world was struggling during the Great Depression, Alaskans did not face the same hard times. Federal government programs funded the first street paving, the building of docks and harbors, and a new city hall in Anchorage. The government also regulated the price of gold, preventing financial ruin for many Alaskans.

World War II had an impact on the lives of all Americans, including those in Alaska. Alaska had key military bases and its proximity to Japan meant it held a critical military position. Troops and supplies came in large numbers by ship. From March to September 1942, the U.S. Army supervised the building of the 1,523-mile-long (2,451 km) Alaska-Canadian Highway,

This city hall building in Anchorage was completed in 1937.

The Alcan Highway spans several types of terrain and many waterways.

## MINI-BIO

### GEORGE T. HARPER: HISTORIAN

Born in Atlanta, Georgia, George T. Harper (1930–2004) centered his life on preserving African American heritage in Alaska. He served in the navy and went to college before becoming a computer programmer. He moved to Anchorage in 1981 and worked for the Bureau of Land Management. In 1989, he created a Black History Month exhibit and three years later, an exhibit honoring black U.S. Army engineers who helped build the Alaska Highway during World War II. With the help of others, he cofounded the Blacks in Alaska History Project to help document the many African American contributions to the state.

 **Want to know more?** See http://consortiumlibrary.org/archives/CollectionsList/CollectionDescriptions/GtoJ/Harpergtbiahp.html

known as the Alcan Highway. It went from Dawson Creek, British Columbia, Canada, to Delta Junction, Alaska. The 97th Engineer Division, half of whom were black troops from the South, built the difficult Alaska section during the region's coldest winter on record and finished ahead of time. In the **segregated** army of the day, many of the brave engineers of the 97th had to live in tents while white soldiers lived in insulated houses.

On June 3, 1942, Japanese bombs landed on Dutch Harbor in the Aleutian Islands. Then Japan's forces

## WORD TO KNOW

**segregated** *separated from others, according to race, class, ethnic group, religion, or other factors*

## ELIZABETH WANAMAKER PERATROVICH: CIVIL RIGHTS CHAMPION

Born into the Tlingit nation, Elizabeth Wanamaker Peratrovich (1911–1958) was raised by missionaries after her parents died. She went to college and then married Roy Peratrovich in 1931. She was deeply troubled by the way Native Alaskans were treated and decided to do something about it. She and her husband lobbied for an antidiscrimination law, and it was her testimony that was the most effective in getting the Alaska Civil Rights Act passed in 1945.

**? Want to know more?** See www.alaskool.org/projects/native_gov/recollections/peratrovich/Honoring_EPeratrovich.htm

When the Japanese invaded the Aleutian Islands, it was the only time that United States soil was occupied by an enemy force since the War of 1812!

took over Attu and Kiska, two Aleutian islands, hoping to divert U.S. troops from more important battles in the Pacific. It took the United States almost a year and more than 200,000 soldiers to regain Attu and Kiska. It was not a pleasant place to wage war. Many soldiers battled frostbite and bitterly cold weather as much as they did enemy forces.

This Aleutian campaign lasted from June 3, 1942, to August 15, 1943. Forty-two Native people on Attu were shipped to Japan as prisoners of war. The United States evacuated the Aleutian Islands, forcing the people from their homes and transporting them to camps in southeast Alaska. Most people had only a moment's notice and were not allowed to take anything with them. Although this was done for their safety, it led to three long years in a new place with too many people and not enough food. Many people died in these camps.

## STATEHOOD AT LAST

World War II brought a great many people to Alaska, and the new highway made it easier to reach the region. Demand for statehood began to grow. In 1955, a constitution for the state was written, which was approved the following year. At last, on January 3, 1959, Alaska became the 49th state in the Union.

# Alaska: From Territory to Statehood

**(1912–1959)**

This map shows the original Alaska territory and the area (outlined in orange) that became the state of Alaska in 1959.

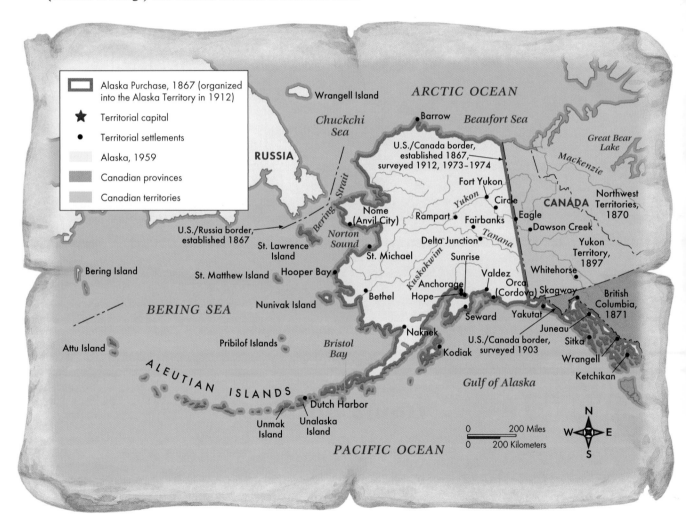

**Legend:**

- Alaska Purchase, 1867 (organized into the Alaska Territory in 1912)
- ★ Territorial capital
- • Territorial settlements
- Alaska, 1959
- Canadian provinces
- Canadian territories

ARCTIC OCEAN

Wrangell Island

*Chuckchi Sea*

Barrow  *Beaufort Sea*

RUSSIA

*Great Bear Lake*

U.S./Canada border, established 1867, surveyed 1912, 1973–1974

*Mackenzie*

Fort Yukon

*Yukon*

Circle

CANADA

Northwest Territories, 1870

U.S./Russia border, established 1867

*Bering Strait*

Nome (Anvil City)

Rampart  Fairbanks

Eagle

Dawson Creek

St. Lawrence Island

*Norton Sound*

St. Michael

Delta Junction  *Tanana*

Yukon Territory, 1897

Bering Island

St. Matthew Island  Hooper Bay

*Kuskokwim*

Sunrise

Anchorage

Valdez

Orca (Cordova)  Skagway

Whitehorse

British Columbia, 1871

*BERING SEA*

Nunivak Island

Bethel  Hope

Seward

Yakutat

Juneau

Attu Island

Pribilof Islands

*Bristol Bay*

Naknek

U.S./Canada border, surveyed 1903

Sitka

Wrangell

*ALEUTIAN ISLANDS*

Kodiak

*Gulf of Alaska*

Ketchikan

Dutch Harbor

Unmak Island

Unalaska Island

*PACIFIC OCEAN*

0    200 Miles
0    200 Kilometers

N
W   E
S

Workers repair the Trans-Alaska pipeline where it crosses the Tanana River.

## THE GOOD FRIDAY EARTHQUAKE

On March 27, 1964, which was Good Friday (the Friday before Easter), an earthquake measuring 9.2 on the Richter scale shook Alaska. It released 10 million times more energy than an atomic bomb and was 80 times more powerful than the 1906 San Francisco earthquake. Amazingly, only 12 people were killed in the quake. But 113 were killed by a tsunami (tidal wave) that followed.

## LIQUID GOLD

As the 1950s ended and the 1960s began, another kind of gold emerged in Alaska. This time it was "liquid gold," or oil. It would transform the Alaskan economy, as well as the state itself. As oil wells were built, more and more jobs were created and money began flowing into the state to be used for building and maintaining roads, new schools, and other improvements. By the early 1970s, Congress passed legislation allowing work to begin on the Trans-Alaska pipeline, a pipeline connecting oil fields in northern Alaska to the port of Valdez in southern Alaska. Construction of the pipeline created even more jobs.

## NATIVE RIGHTS

Since statehood, Native Alaskans had been concerned about the claiming and distribution of land. The discovery of oil at Prudhoe Bay in northern Alaska added

Thousands marched in downtown Anchorage in 2002, protesting a court decision affecting the rights of Alaska Natives.

## FLOOD!

The summer of 1967 was different from most in Fairbanks. Rather than hot and dry, this summer was hot and wet. It rained often, so much that the ground was unable to absorb the water. In August, it began raining again—and then pouring. The roads into the city were soon flooded. In the early morning hours of August 14, Fairbanks residents awoke to the sound of sirens and water rushing into their homes through doors and windows. The Chena River had overflowed its banks! Thousands of people had to be rescued from their homes by boat. They were not able to return home for a week until the floodwaters finally receded.

urgency to the process of declaring land rights, and the U.S. Congress passed the Alaskan Native Claims Settlement Act in 1971. Native Alaskans were granted 44 million acres (18 million hectares) of land and paid $962.5 million in exchange for any future claims to the other 331 millions acres (134 million ha) of Alaskan land. The total area of the lands given to Native groups equals that of the entire state of Washington. This settlement gave Native Alaskans the land they needed to continue their traditional lifestyles.

The following year, the Marine Mammal Protection Act was passed, which included a provision allowing Native people to continue to hunt otherwise restricted marine animals. In 1978, an organization called the Alaska Eskimo Whaling Commission was formed to preserve the rights of Alaska's Native people to hunt bowhead whales. Later, in 2001, the governor issued an executive order called the Millennium Agreement, stating that the government would begin consulting Native groups before making decisions affecting Alaska.

Hunters in an umiak look for bowhead whales

A moose crosses a street in downtown Anchorage.

## LOOKING TOWARD THE FUTURE

As the 21st century began, Alaska faced many challenges. Among the key issues Alaskans must address are the preservation of the state's Native heritage and the protection of its natural environment.

## DISASTER STRIKES

On March 24, 1989, an Exxon Corporation (today ExxonMobile) oil tanker, the *Exxon Valdez,* hit a reef in Prince William Sound, spilling 11 million gallons (42 million liters) of oil. It was one of the worst human-caused disasters in history. The oil killed seabirds, otters, harbor seals, and eagles. Thousands more animals were coated in oil, as were the rocky coves of Prince William Sound.

A red necked grebe covered in oil after the *Exxon Valdez* spill

# READ ABOUT

A participant in the 2007 World Eskimo-Indian Olympics in Anchorage is lofted into the air in the blanket toss. Alaska Natives used to fling whale spotters into the air in a similar style.

# CHAPTER SIX

# PEOPLE

ECAUSE OF ALASKA'S IMMENSE SIZE AND SMALL POPULATION, MANY PEOPLE IN RURAL AREAS LIVE MILES AND MILES APART FROM THEIR NEIGHBORS. Most Alaskans choose to live in the state's largest cities of Anchorage, Fairbanks, and Juneau.

Alaska Natives march through downtown Juneau during a parade celebrating their cultures.

## A MIX OF CULTURES

Alaska's Native people have fought hard to preserve and protect their traditional ways of life. In 1971, the Alaska Native Claims Settlement Act (ANCSA) was passed, officially recognizing Native claims to land. Over time, Native cultures, traditions, and languages have been brought back and revived for the newest generations to learn and someday pass on. But there is a constant struggle between cen-

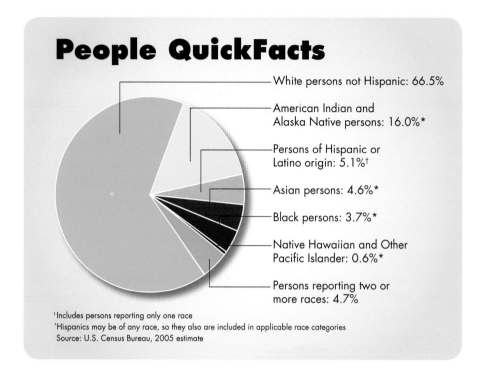

# People QuickFacts

- White persons not Hispanic: 66.5%
- American Indian and Alaska Native persons: 16.0%*
- Persons of Hispanic or Latino origin: 5.1%†
- Asian persons: 4.6%*
- Black persons: 3.7%*
- Native Hawaiian and Other Pacific Islander: 0.6%*
- Persons reporting two or more races: 4.7%

†Includes persons reporting only one race
*Hispanics may be of any race, so they also are included in applicable race categories
Source: U.S. Census Bureau, 2005 estimate

turies-old traditions and the lure of the modern world. Many young Native Alaskans try to blend the two. For example, in 1988, 2,000 Inupiaqs living on the north coast gathered in Barrow. They were there to celebrate *kevgiq*, the messenger feast. They had not celebrated it for 70 years! At the festival, gifts were exchanged and foods were prepared, including traditional dishes made with whale meat. The sounds of storytelling, drumming, and dancing filled the air. Since then, the event has been held every year.

Some African Americans in Alaska today are descendents of seafarers who arrived on whaling ships or explorers who went during the gold rush. Others may be related to the many African American military engineers who helped build the Alaskan-Canadian Highway. More than 3,000 African Americans arrived during World War II and stayed.

## WORD TO KNOW

**canneries** *factories where food is canned*

# Big-City Life

This list shows the population of Alaska's biggest cities.

**Anchorage** . . . . . . . . . .278,700
**Fairbanks** . . . . . . . . . . . .31,142
**Juneau** . . . . . . . . . . . . . .30,737
**Wasilla** . . . . . . . . . . . . . .9,236
**Sitka** . . . . . . . . . . . . . . . .8,920

Source: U.S. Census Bureau, 2006 estimate

Today, Alaska's Asian American population includes Filipinos, Koreans, Chinese, Japanese, and Thais. Some are descendants of immigrants who went to work in the gold mines or in the **canneries**. The largest Asian American group in Alaska today is Filipinos. They first arrived in Alaska in the 1700s. They arrived to work as crew members on fur trading vessels and later on whaling ships. Other people arrived from the Philippines later to work building underwater communication cables.

Members of the Filipino Visayan Association of the Kodiak Ensemble perform in a Filipino celebration in 2006.

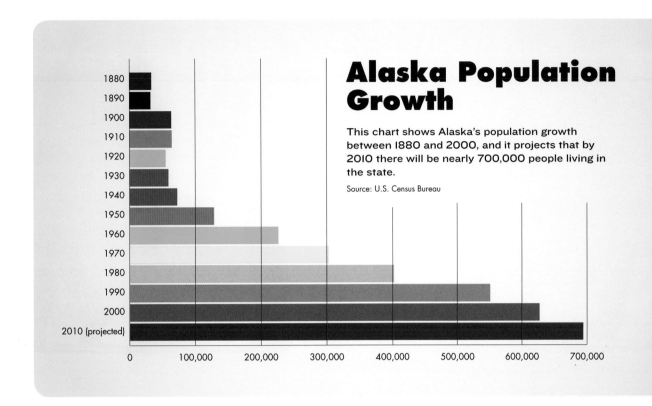

## Alaska Population Growth

This chart shows Alaska's population growth between 1880 and 2000, and it projects that by 2010 there will be nearly 700,000 people living in the state.

Source: U.S. Census Bureau

## EDUCATION

When it comes to education, Alaska has come a long way. Before 1976, there were no high schools in the state's most remote villages. Students had to attend boarding schools in the larger cities or out of state. Today, Alaska has 500 public schools. They vary in size from large schools with several thousand students to much smaller ones with only a couple dozen students. Some young people in Alaska are homeschooled. In a program that started in 1939, lessons were initially delivered by mail and later by satellite. Now lessons arrive over the Internet. Students can view lectures and classes on television or on their computers. They study, do their homework, and then turn in their lessons either by mail

Students at the University of Alaska in Anchorage walk to class.

or electronically. Alaska's high school graduation rate is well below the national average, but improvements continue to be made in the state's education system to encourage kids to stay in school.

One-quarter of Alaskan adults have college degrees. There are a number of colleges and universities in the state, including Alaska Pacific University and Matanuska-Susitna College, both in Anchorage. The University of Alaska has campuses in Anchorage, Fairbanks, and Juneau. All offer four-year bachelors degrees, as well as graduate degrees. In the past, many high school graduates left Alaska. The state knew it had to do something to keep graduates in the state. It started a program that awards money toward college tuition at state universities for the top 10 percent of each high school graduating class.

# Where Alaskans Live

The colors on this map indicate population density throughout the state.
The darker the color, the more people live there.

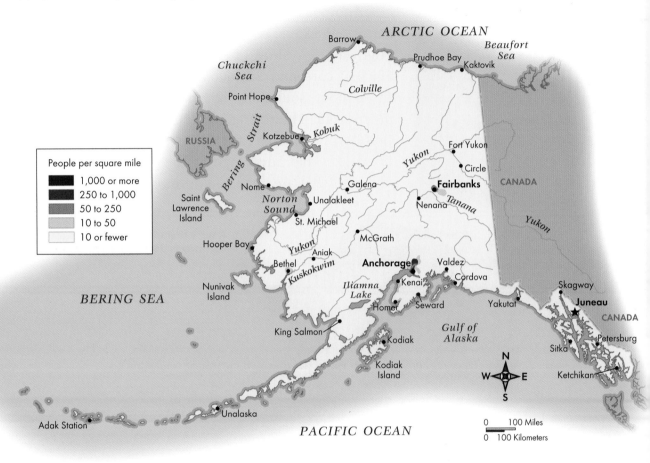

## GETTING FROM PLACE TO PLACE

With few roads and a lot of land, how do Alaskans get from one place to another? The only paved road that goes in and out of the state is the Alaska Highway. In rural towns, more often than not, a paved road will lead to a dead end. Cars just are not that helpful in remote villages and extreme weather conditions! Instead, people in rural areas rely on all-terrain vehicles (ATVs)

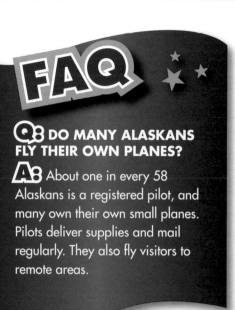

# FAQ

**Q8 DO MANY ALASKANS FLY THEIR OWN PLANES?**

**A8** About one in every 58 Alaskans is a registered pilot, and many own their own small planes. Pilots deliver supplies and mail regularly. They also fly visitors to remote areas.

that can travel over almost any type of ground. Other modes of transportation include old-fashioned dog-sleds, modern snowmobiles, and small airplanes.

Another convenient way to travel in Alaska is over water. Alaskans commonly use the Alaska Marine Highway, a system of ferries that carries more than 100,000 cars and 350,000 people each year to ports throughout southeast, south-central, and southwestern Alaska. The ferries cover 3,500 miles (5,600 km). Because many trips can take more than a day, travelers in Alaska take advantage of the cabins with showers and beds that are available on most ships.

A ferry that is part of the Alaska Marine Highway is docked in southeast Alaska.

Musician Mary Youngblood holds her Grammy Award for Best Native American Music Album in 2003.

## THE SOUND OF MUSIC

Alaskans listen to much of the same music as people in the Lower 48. But some music you hear in Alaska traces its roots to Native Alaskan traditions. Flutist Mary Youngblood, for example, is popular in Alaska. Youngblood is half Seminole and half Aleut. She wanted to learn how to play the music that was part of her heritage so she studies flute, guitar, piano, and voice. Youngblood was featured in two PBS documentaries, bringing her music to the attention of a larger audience. She has released five CDs to date. The title of her 1997 album, *Dance with the Wind*, was inspired by the sight of trees bending and swaying during a storm.

Another popular Alaskan musician is Libby Roderick. Her folk songs of peace and compassion have been performed at political conferences from Washington, D.C., to Beijing, China. She received a citation from the Alaska legislature for her music and her passion for important issues such as world peace and the preservation of the wilderness. She is best known for her song "How Could Anyone," which has been translated into multiple languages and performed by many different artists.

One of the most popular groups in Alaska is Pamya, a four-member Yup'ik group from Anchorage. The musicians call their music "tribal funk," and much of it is performed in the Native languages. The group has toured around the world and throughout the United States with a goal to "share the ancient stories of [its] people through music and dance." In 2003, their recording *Caught*

Libby Roderick singing at her home in Anchorage

*in the Act* won record of the year at the Native American Music Awards.

Many music lovers head to Juneau each April for the annual Alaska Folk Festival. The event began in 1975 when six folk musicians from the area decided to perform at the Alaska State Museum for the fun of it. Since then, it has grown and attracted some of the best-known folk musicians from around the world.

## ALASKAN LITERATURE

Velma Wallis was forced to drop out of school at the age of 13. Her father had died, and she was needed at home to take care of her brothers and sisters. She earned her high school diploma by taking the General Education Development test, or GED. Then, once her siblings were older, she moved to an old trapping cabin outside Fort Yukon. For more than ten years, she lived there, surviving on only what she could hunt, fish, or trap. There she wrote *Two Old Women*, which won the Western States book award in 1993. She is also the author of *Bird Girl and the Man Who Followed the Sun* and *Raising Ourselves*.

Alaska's stunning natural environment has inspired many writers. One such writer was Jack London. His motto in life was, "I shall not waste my days in trying to prolong them—I shall use my time." He was an adventurer as well as an author. London went to Alaska in

**MINI-BIO**

### JEWEL KILCHER: MUSICAL ARTIST

Jewel Kilcher (1974– ) moved to Alaska as a child. By age 6, she was singing for tourists and even yodeling! For years, Jewel sang in small clubs. Finally, in 1994 she recorded her first album. Within a year, she had a half-dozen hit singles. In addition to being a popular singer, she has also acted in films and published books of poetry. Some of her biggest hits include "Pieces of You" and "Foolish Games."

**?  Want to know more?** See www.nps.gov/home/historyculture/upload/MW,pdf,KilcherBio,b.pdf

## DEB VANASSE: TEACHER AND AUTHOR

Deb Vanasse (1957–) was born in St. Paul, Minnesota. She and her family moved often when she was young. She graduated from Bemidji State University and decided to teach in Alaska. She began in Nunapitchuk and later moved to Bethel. Her experiences inspired her to write *A Distant Enemy.* After moving to Fairbanks in 1987, she wrote *Out of the Wilderness.* Since then, she has written a number of children's books about Alaska, including *Under Alaska's Midnight Sun,* *Alaska Animal Babies,* and *A Totem Tale.*

**? Want to know more?**
See www.debvanasse.com

The Alaskan wilderness inspired Jack London to write *Call of the Wild* and other books.

1898 to search for gold and spent a great deal of time in the region. His classic novel *Call of the Wild* is about a pet dog from California who becomes a sled dog in the Yukon and Alaska during the gold rush.

## ALASKAN ENTERTAINERS

Alaskan entertainers have starred in television shows and in films. Irene Bedard was the voice of Pocahontas in the Disney film of the same name. Ray Mala was one of the first successful Native American actors. He

Actor Ray Mala appeared in more that 25 films and also worked as a cameraman.

typically was cast as Alaska Native or Hawaiian characters in the 25-plus films in which he appeared. In 1925, Mala went to Hollywood and became a cameraman for Fox Films. He starred in a silent film called *Eskimo*. It won the first ever Academy Award for Best Film Editing.

## MINI-BIO

### IRENE BEDARD: ACTRESS

Irene Bedard (1967—) is part Creek Indian and part Inupiaq. She has starred in a number of movies and television shows including *Lakota Woman*, *Squanto*, and *Wildflowers*. She provided the voice for the main character in Disney's *Pocahontas* and has also done voices for *The Real Adventures of Johnny Quest* and *Pepper Ann*. She lived in Alaska until the age of eight before moving to Washington State.

**? Want to know more?**
See www.irenebedardanddeni.com/home.html

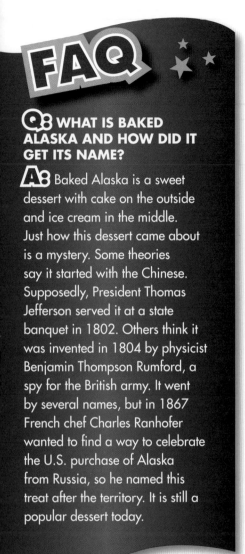

## FAQ

### Q8 WHAT IS BAKED ALASKA AND HOW DID IT GET ITS NAME?

**A8** Baked Alaska is a sweet dessert with cake on the outside and ice cream in the middle. Just how this dessert came about is a mystery. Some theories say it started with the Chinese. Supposedly, President Thomas Jefferson served it at a state banquet in 1802. Others think it was invented in 1804 by physicist Benjamin Thompson Rumford, a spy for the British army. It went by several names, but in 1867 French chef Charles Ranhofer wanted to find a way to celebrate the U.S. purchase of Alaska from Russia, so he named this treat after the territory. It is still a popular dessert today.

## HOW TO TALK LIKE AN ALASKAN

If you want to sound like a local Alaskan, try using these words and phrases:

*break up:* when the ice begins to thaw and break apart

*the bush:* places in Alaska not connected to anywhere by roads

*cabin fever:* the way you feel (restless and cooped up) after you spend too much time indoors during the long period when there is no sunlight

*cheechako:* a newcomer to Alaska

*ice fog:* a thick winter fog made out of ice particles that cling to tree branches

*mukluks:* soft, warm boots that go high up the leg

*Outside:* the 48 states of the continental United States

*sourdough:* an Alaskan old timer or, more generally, a person who has spent a winter in Alaska

To sound like a Native Alaskan, you also need to know all of the words that locals use to describe snow. For example,

*apun:* fallen snow on the ground

*muruaneq:* deep fallen snow on the ground

*nutaryuk:* fresh snow

*qanisqineq:* snow floating on water

*qanuk:* snowflake

*qengaruk:* snowbank

## HOW TO EAT LIKE AN ALASKAN

Alaska is a seafood lover's paradise! In Alaska, you will find salmon, the state fish, served at breakfast, lunch, and dinner. And crab, too! Alaskan menus often include kinds of meat that may be unfamiliar to "outsiders," such as moose and caribou.

Salmon burger

# MENU

## WHAT'S ON THE MENU IN ALASKA?

★ ★ ★

### Halibut Tempura

Pieces of fish dipped in batter and deep-fried.

### Alaskan King Crab

King crabs are fished in Alaska, in the freezing waters of the Bering Sea. Alaskan crab fishing is one of the most dangerous jobs in the United States. In fact, the television show *Deadliest Catch* features king crab fishers at work.

### Salmon

Salmon is the state fish of Alaska. It is enjoyed at any meal and can be served in many ways. No matter how it's prepared, it's delicious and nutritious.

### Brownie Alaska

Strawberry ice cream covering a nutty brownie.

### Eskimo Ice Cream

*Akutaq*, also known as Eskimo ice cream, is a traditional dish that could once be found throughout Alaska. It was typically made using berries, animal oil, dried fat, fish, and eggs. A modern variation is made with vegetable shortening, sugar, dried fruit, and frozen berries.

### TRY THIS RECIPE
### Alaskan Cranberry Cake

Try out this recipe and share it with friends. Have a grown-up nearby to help.

**Ingredients:**
1 ½ cups sugar
2 eggs
¾ cup butter, melted and cooled
¼ cup maple syrup
2 teaspoons almond extract
1 ½ cups flour
½ cup chopped pecans
½ cup chopped hazelnuts
2 cups cranberries

**Instructions:**
1. Preheat oven to 350°F.
2. Grease a 9 x 13 inch baking dish.
3. Beat together sugar and eggs until fluffy.
4. Add melted butter, almond extract, and maple syrup. Mix well.
5. Stir in flour, pecans, and hazelnuts.
6. Gently fold in the cranberries.
7. Pour batter into pan and bake for one hour.

Alaskan king crab

## SPORTS AND ATHLETES

Alaska has produced a number of top athletes over the years. Among them are Iditarod mushers (drivers of dogsled teams). The state sport, after all, is dog mushing. The Iditarod Trail Sled Dog Race, which began in 1967, was the idea of Dorothy Page. In the 1920s, settlers and gold rushers arriving on the Alaska coast used what became known as the Iditarod Trail to reach inland gold fields. At that time, the only way to travel over this rugged land was by dogsled. The trail was also used to deliver the mail and supplies, as well as by

Jon Little of Kasilof drives his team out of the starting chute in the 2003 Iditarod Trail Sled Dog Race.

Libby Riddles celebrates with two of her dogs following her Iditarod win in 1985.

people traveling from village to village. Later, as travel by airplane and snowmobile became more common, people no longer traveled by dogsled.

In celebration of Alaska's centennial in 1967, Page and Joe Reddington, known as the Father of the Iditarod, organized the first Iditarod dogsled race. That race, and another in 1969, followed only part of the Iditarod Trail. Then, in 1973, the race was extended to Nome, a journey of about 1,150 miles (1,850 km).

Today, the race is an annual event. Mushers from all over the world go to Alaska to compete. The trip takes between 9 and 12 days to complete and only the most skilled and rugged mushers and highly trained sled dogs can endure such a challenging race.

Libby Riddles was the first woman to win the Last Great Race on Earth, as the Iditarod is sometimes called. She won it in 1985 at the age of 29. After her

An athlete performs the One Hand Reach during the 2006 Senior Native Youth Olympic Games in Anchorage.

came Susan Butcher, the only woman to win the race three years in a row.

One of Alaska's unique sporting events is the World Eskimo-Indian Olympics. First held in 1961, this annual event is open only to Alaska Natives. The games honor Native heritage. Some events test strength, while others measure agility.

Olympic medal winners who have trained or lived for a time in Alaska include Hilary Lindh and Tommy Moe, both medalists in downhill skiing (1992 and 1994, respectively). Scott Gomez was born in Anchorage. He was the National Hockey League's Rookie of the Year in 2000. Alaska's semiprofessional hockey team, the Anchorage Aces, won the Kelly Cup in 2006.

Alaska's first professional football team was organized in 2006. Called the Alaska Wild, the team chose its name from more than 1,500 suggestions submitted by fans. As part of the Intense Football League, the team won its first ever game on July 5, 2007. It was also the first professional football victory in the history of Alaska!

Alaskans know that in many ways, life in the Last Frontier is different from life in the Lower 48. Alaskans welcome newcomers to their land. They know it takes an enduring and dedicated spirit to call Alaska home.

Alaska native Scott Gomez hits the ice as a member of the New Jersey Devils hockey team.

# READ ABOUT

Voters line up at
a polling place in
Anchorage during
the 2004 election.

# CHAPTER SEVEN

# GOVERNMENT

★

WORKING TO PRESERVE ALASKA'S NATURAL BEAUTY IS IMPORTANT TO THE PEOPLE WHO LIVE THERE, AND THEY SHOW THEIR CONCERN BY PASSING LAWS THAT PROTECT THE ENVIRONMENT. For example, in 1998, Alaskans voted to keep their state "forever free" of billboards. "Alaskans and tourists alike enjoy a drive through fantastic scenery, not a drive through the Yellow Pages," wrote one resident to the local newspaper.

# Capitol Facts

Here are some fascinating facts about Alaska's state capitol.

**Ground broken** . . . . . . .September 18, 1929
**Completed** . . . . . . . . . . . . February 2, 1931
**Dedicated** . . . . . . . . . . . . February 14, 1931
**Height** . . . . . . . . . . . . . . . . . . . . . .Six stories
**Exterior** . . . . . . Brick-faced reinforced concrete
and Indiana limestone. Four marble
columns from Prince of Wales Island
**Location** . . . . . . . . . . . . . . . . . . . . . . .Juneau

## GATEWAY TO THE GLACIERS

Juneau may be one of the most unusual capital cities in the United States. There are no roads leading into it. To get there, you have to fly in or take a ferry. Because it is so close to a number of glaciers, the city is also known as the Gateway to the Glaciers. Alaskans have long debated whether the capital should be relocated to a less remote city. In 1976, they voted to move it to Willow, a more central location. But they changed their minds when they discovered it would cost more than $2 billion to do so. When the vote came up again in 2002, Alaskans said no thanks.

The state capitol in Juneau

# Capital City

This map shows places of interest in Juneau, Alaska's capital city.

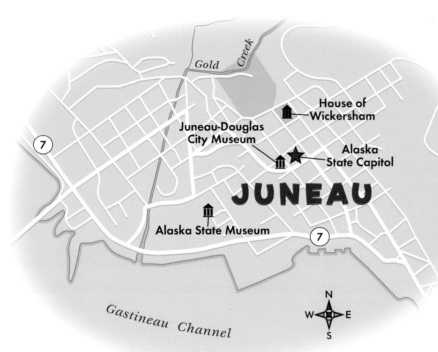

**Gold Creek**

**7**

**House of Wickersham**

**Juneau-Douglas City Museum**

**Alaska State Capitol**

# JUNEAU

**Alaska State Museum**

**7**

**Gastineau Channel**

N W E S

## WOW

In 1980, President Jimmy Carter signed the Alaska National Interest Lands Conservation Act, adding 80 million acres (32 million ha) of public lands and wilderness areas in Alaska.

## THE STATE CONSTITUTION

To prepare for statehood, Alaska had to create a constitution. In 1955, Alaska held a constitutional convention at the University of Alaska Fairbanks, in what has been renamed Constitution Hall. Alaska had the advantage of having 48 other state constitutions to review as examples. The 55 delegates from around the territory crafted a very short document (just 1,400 words) that set up the structure and procedures for the future state. The voters approved the constitution the following year, and statehood came in 1959.

## SEE IT HERE!

### MOUNT ROBERTS TRAMWAY

For a unique way to see Alaska's capital, take a ride on the Mount Roberts Tramway. Climb into a cable car that takes you 1,800 feet (550 m) above the city. At the tramway station, you can see displays of Native artwork, have a quick bite to eat, or even go to the theater. The tramway is one of the most popular attractions in Alaska, drawing more than 200,000 tourists a year.

## WILLIAM EGAN: FIRST GOVERNOR

When Alaska became a state in 1959, its first governor was William Egan (1914–1984). He served two terms (1959–1966 and 1970–1974) and is considered one of the "modern fathers" of Alaska. He helped hold Alaska together after the devastating Good Friday earthquake in 1964.

**? Want to know more?** See *Alaska's Homegrown Governor: A Biography of William A. Egan*, by Elizabeth Tower (Anchorage, AK: Publication Consultants, 2003).

Since statehood, new issues have led to several revisions of the constitution. These issues include the protection of natural resources, economic development, and historic preservation. The Alaska Constitution favors a strong governor. It also divides the state government into three branches: executive, legislative, and judicial.

# Alaska's State Government

## EXECUTIVE BRANCH
Carries out state laws

Governor

Lt. Governor

Department heads for
Corrections
Health and Social Services
Environmental Conservation
Labor and Workforce
Development
and many more

## LEGISLATIVE BRANCH
Makes and passes state laws

Senate
(20 members)

House of
Representatives
(40 members)

## JUDICIAL BRANCH
Enforces state laws

Supreme
Court

Superior
Courts

Court of
Appeals

District
Courts

These candidates for governor debate the issues in 2006 (from left, Andrew Halcro, Sarah Palin, and Tony Knowles).

## THE EXECUTIVE BRANCH

The executive branch carries out the state laws, which are created by the legislature. The governor is the head of the executive branch, and the lieutenant governor serves in the event the governor cannot finish his or her term. The governor and lieutenant governor are elected to four-year terms. The governor appoints state officials, such as the attorney general, district attorneys, and judges.

# Representing Alaska

This list shows the number of elected officials who represent Alaska, on both the state and national levels.

| OFFICE | NUMBER | LENGTH OF TERM |
|---|---|---|
| **State senators** | 20 | 4 years |
| **State representatives** | 40 | 4 years |
| **U.S. senators** | 2 | 6 years |
| **U.S. representatives** | 1 | 2 years |
| **Presidential electors** | 3 | — |

## SARAH PALIN: YOUNGEST GOVERNOR

In 2006, Sarah Palin (1964–) became the first female and the youngest governor of Alaska. She was born in Idaho but came to Alaska when she was a baby. Until she entered politics, Palin worked in media. She began her political career as mayor of Wasilla. In that role, she reduced taxes and worked to bring new business to the area. She is married to Todd Palin, three-time champion of the Iron Dog, the world's longest snow machine race. Palin serves on the Oil and Gas Compact Commission, and she says her priorities are education, public safety, and transportation.

❓ **Want to know more?** See www.gov.state.ak.us/

# THE LEGISLATIVE BRANCH

Alaska's legislative branch is divided into the senate and the house of representatives. In the senate, 20 state senators serve four-year terms. In the house, 40 representatives serve two-year terms. Members of the legislature make state laws and approve the budget.

Delegates to the Conference on Alaskans vote on amendments to the state constitution in 2004.

## THE JUDICIAL BRANCH

The judicial branch upholds state laws through the court system. There are four levels in the court system: the supreme court, the court of appeals, superior courts, and district courts.

## LOCAL GOVERNMENT

One-third of Alaska is divided into 16 boroughs. The other two-thirds of the state has no organized local government and instead is controlled by the state government. There are also 246 federally recognized tribal governments in Alaska.

Senator Georgianna Lincoln wearing Native dress in the state senate, May 2004.

## WEIRD AND WACKY LAWS

Alaska has some pretty strange laws. Here are a few:

- Moose may not be viewed from an airplane.
- Waking a sleeping bear for the purpose of taking its picture is prohibited.
- It is an offense to push a live moose out of a moving airplane.

# Alaska Boroughs

This map shows the 16 boroughs in Alaska. Juneau, the state capital, is indicated with a star.

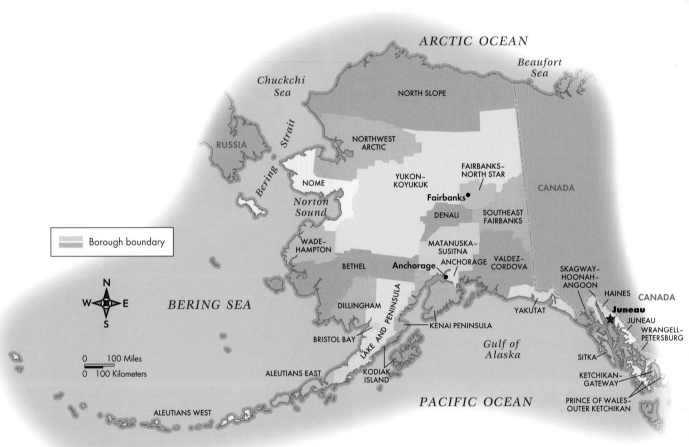

## KIDS MAKING A DIFFERENCE

There is an old saying that goes, "You can't fight city hall." This means a single person cannot make much of a difference in government. But Molly Hootch's story is the perfect example to prove the statement wrong! In 1976, when she was 16 years old, Hootch and other

Thanks to Molly Hootch's efforts, hundreds of Alaskan villages have high schools. Here, students learn about Native beadwork.

students in her class won a lawsuit against the Alaska Board of Education. Known now as the Molly Hootch Decree, the court instructed the state to provide a high school in any community that has at least 15 high-school-age young people. Immediately, more than 100 of the state's smallest villages became eligible.

# State Flag

In 1926, the American Legion, an organization of U.S. veterans, held a contest for students in grades 7 to 12 to design a flag for the Territory of Alaska. The selection committee was captivated by the simplicity, elegance, and appropriateness of 13-year-old Benny Benson's design: the golden Big Dipper and North Star on a dark blue background.

Benson was a young Native Alaskan living at the mission school in Seward when he created his award-winning design. The Legion asked the territorial government to adopt his design as the official territorial flag, which it did. The same flag was later adopted as the state flag. Today, a main street in Anchorage is named Benson Boulevard in honor of the flag's designer.

# State Seal

The state seal was originally designed in 1910 before Alaska became a state. The rays above the mountains represent the northern lights. The smelter symbolizes mining. The train stands for Alaska's railroads, and ships represents transportation by sea. The trees symbolize Alaska's wealth of forests, and the farmer, his horse, and the three shocks of wheat represent Alaskan agriculture. The fish and the seals signify the importance of fishing and wildlife to Alaska's economy.

## READ ABOUT

Alaska's natural
beauty lures
many tourists
to the state,
especially during
the summer.

CHAPTER EIGHT

# ECONOMY

★

THANKS TO ABUNDANT NATURAL RESOURCES, THERE ARE FIVE TIMES MORE JOBS IN ALASKA TODAY THAN THERE WERE IN 1961. Two major Alaska industries, oil and fishing, have faced ups and downs over the years. But one area of industry has grown steadily: tourism. Along with tourists have come jobs for Alaskans.

A commercial fishing crew unload their catch of salmon.

**The activity on board a fishing ship is nonstop. Once caught, the fish must be quickly cleaned, filleted, packaged, and frozen. It is time to go home only when the ships' freezers cannot hold any more fish.**

## LIFE ON THE SEA

One of Alaska's oldest industries is fishing. Alaska produces more seafood than any other state in the country, pulling in more than 5 billion pounds (2.3 billion kilograms) of it each year. Although the season typically lasts just a few months, it is hectic. Many fish can be caught only during the summer. Red king crab may be fished only a few days out of the whole year, so fishers scramble to make sure their traps are in place on those days! Salmon, herring, halibut, and shrimp must be caught while they are plentiful in Alaska's oceans. To make the most of the season, many fishers spend two to three months at a time on a ship. They can make a good profit only if they remain at sea until their ships are completely full.

# What Do Alaskans Do?

This color-coded chart shows what industries Alaskans work in.

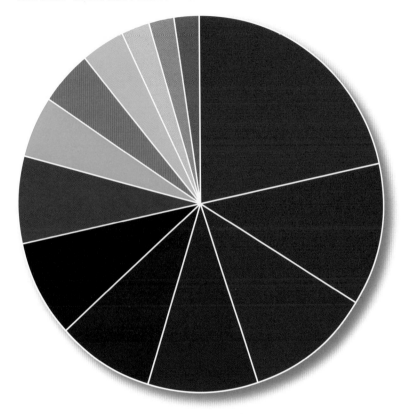

**21.7%** Educational services, health care, and social assistance, 65,515

**12.2%** Retail trade, 36,867

**11.3%** Public administration, 34,198

**9.7%** Construction, 29,384

**8.6%** Transportation, warehousing, and utilities, 25,942

**8.3%** Arts, entertainment, recreation, accommodation, and food services, 25,051

**7.5%** Professional, scientific, management, administrative and waste management services, 22,672

**5.3%** Other services, except public administration, 15,980

**4.8%** Finance insurance, real estate, and rental and leasing, 14,452

**3.7%** Agriculture, forestry, fishing and hunting, and mining, 11,119

**2.6%** Information, 7,990

**2.2%** Manufacturing, 6,680

**2.1%** Wholesale trade, 6,457

*Source: U.S. Census Bureau, 2000*

## ANOTHER ALASKAN TREASURE

For years, Alaska had proved to be full of valuable resources—from abundant animals and plants to gold. In the late 1960s, another resource was discovered: oil! In 1968, oil was found on the North Slope of Prudhoe

Oil drilling is a mainstay of Alaska's economy, particularly on the North Slope.

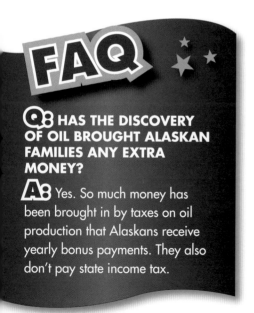

# FAQ

**Q8 HAS THE DISCOVERY OF OIL BROUGHT ALASKAN FAMILIES ANY EXTRA MONEY?**

**A8** Yes. So much money has been brought in by taxes on oil production that Alaskans receive yearly bonus payments. They also don't pay state income tax.

Bay. In fact, it was the largest oil field discovered in North America. The question was how to transport the oil from 300 miles (480 km) north of the Arctic Circle to a port on the Gulf of Alaska. The solution was the Trans-Alaska Pipeline System, a pipe that carries oil both underground and aboveground for 800 miles (1,300 km) across three mountain ranges and hundreds of rivers and streams. Building the pipeline not only became a way to move the oil, but it also provided hundreds of jobs. Many people traveled to Alaska to work on the pipeline, expanding the state's population.

Although building the pipeline cost billions of dollars, Alaska's taxes on oil production brought in even more money. This provided the state with the money to build schools and improve roads. Today, about 85 cents of every dollar the state makes comes from oil.

## BEYOND OIL

The demand for oil has remained strong throughout the state's history. But oil isn't the only natural resource found in the ground in Alaska. Alaska is the world's largest producer of zinc, which is often used in cosmetics, vitamin supplements, and construction materials. Gold, silver, coal, copper, tin, and mercury can be found in the state as well.

Miners drill for silver in southeastern Alaska at the Greens Creek Mine in the Tongass National Forest.

## AUSTIN EUGENE LATHROP: MILLIONAIRE

Austin Eugene "Cap" Lathrop (1865–1950) went to Alaska at the start of the gold rush. Soon he was taking prospectors and their supplies to and from Alaska on his own steamship. Throughout his life, he held a number of odd jobs, from drilling for oil to owning a movie theater. In later life, he opened several radio stations in Alaska. Although he was eventually quite successful, he was not a fan of the idea of statehood. He thought it would bring taxes and laws to the area that would hurt businesses like his.

**? Want to know more?** See www.alaska.edu/opa/eInfo/index.xml?StoryID=245

# Top Products

**Agriculture** poultry, hogs, sheep, lambs, salmon, halibut, herring, red king crab, shrimp, eggs, milk, barley, hay, oats, and potatoes

**Manufacturing** food processing, mining, fish products, refined oil

**Mining** petroleum, gold, zinc, silver, copper, tin, mercury, coal, crushed stone, lead, and sand and gravel

## AGRICULTURE

Alaska has an abundance of land, but farming is a difficult business in Alaska. With the state's small population, farmers do not have a large enough market to support widespread agriculture. It is more cost effective to import most of the state's food than to grow it locally. There are about 500 farms in Alaska, which produce mainly eggs, milk, potatoes, summer vegetables, barley, hay, and oats.

# Major Agricultural and Mining Products

This map shows where Alaska's major agricultural and mining products come from. See potatoes? That means potatoes are grown there.

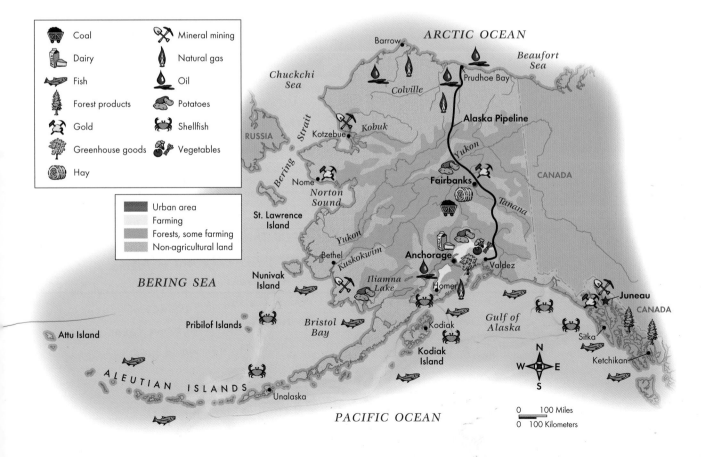

## LOOKING IN NEW DIRECTIONS

In 1985, world oil prices plunged, dramatically reducing Alaska's wealth. Over the next few years, many people lost their jobs, businesses failed, and the economy suffered. Alaska's population began to decline, and in one year alone more than 30,000 people left Anchorage seeking work elsewhere. Clearly, the state had to find a way to help its people. Tourism and fishing both began to expand.

Today, tourism is a growth industry in Alaska. In 2006, more than 1.63 million people visited this huge state. Many tourists sailed in on cruise ships. Others came to fish and camp in the vast national parks. Travelers known as **ecotourists** journey to Alaska to enjoy its many pristine wilderness areas and natural wonders. To support these tourists, businesses that cater to visitors grew, providing many new jobs. From hotels and restaurants to wilderness adventure tours and flightseeing excursions, the service industry expanded. More people and more businesses mean more support services such as hospitals and banks, retail stores and law firms. Of course, not all of the more than $1.5 billion tourists spend on food, lodging, supplies, and entertainment stays in Alaska. Much of it goes to parent companies headquartered outside of the state. Many Alaskans work in the tourism industry for part of the year.

With its plentiful oil reserves, abundant fish and seafood, and thriving tourist and service industries, Alaska's economy has the potential for a bright future.

### WORD TO KNOW

**ecotourists** *people who travel to a place to see unique natural sites*

Tourists taking in the view of Denali

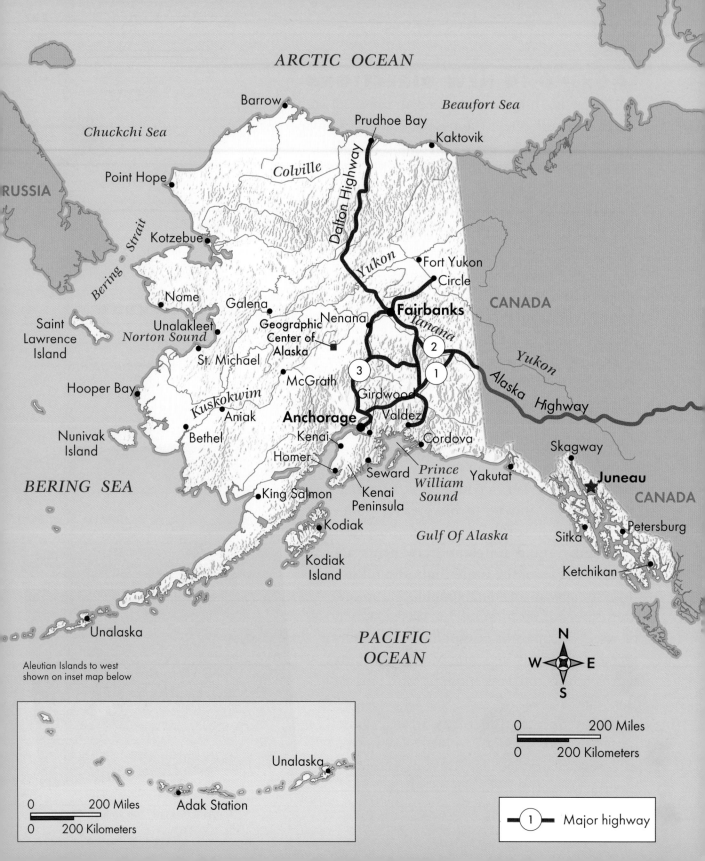

ARCTIC OCEAN

*Chuckchi Sea*

*Beaufort Sea*

Barrow

Prudhoe Bay

Kaktovik

RUSSIA

Point Hope

*Colville*

Dalton Highway

*Yukon*

Kotzebue

Fort Yukon

Circle

CANADA

Nome

Galena

Nenana

**Fairbanks**

Saint
Lawrence
Island

*Norton Sound*

Unalakleet

Geographic
Center of
Alaska

*Tanana*

②

*Yukon*

St. Michael

③

①

*Alaska*

Hooper Bay

McGrath

*Highway*

*Kuskokwim*

Girdwood

Nunivak
Island

Aniak

**Anchorage**

Valdez

Bethel

Kenai

Cordova

Skagway

**BERING SEA**

Homer

Seward

*Prince
William
Sound*

Yakutat

**Juneau**

King Salmon

Kenai
Peninsula

CANADA

Kodiak

Sitka

Petersburg

Kodiak
Island

*Gulf Of Alaska*

Ketchikan

Unalaska

PACIFIC
OCEAN

N

W · E

S

Aleutian Islands to west
shown on inset map below

0          200 Miles

0          200 Kilometers

Unalaska

Adak Station

0     200 Miles

0     200 Kilometers

①━━ Major highway

# CHAPTER NINE

# TRAVEL GUIDE

★

YOU'LL WANT TO SET ASIDE PLENTY OF TIME FOR A VISIT TO ALASKA. It's a huge place with a lot to see and do. From modern cities to towering glaciers, from endless stretches of tundra to some of the highest mountain peaks in the world, you'll be dazzled by all that Alaska has to offer. So grab your map and let's go sightseeing!

← Follow along with this travel map. We'll begin in Juneau and travel all the way to Barrow!

# INSIDE PASSAGE

**THINGS TO DO:** Gawk at one of the biggest glaciers in the world, watch a Native Alaskan dance, and pretend you're an eagle.

## Juneau

★ **Alaska State Museum:** Here you'll learn all about the state's history. You can climb a circular staircase to the top of a tree to see an eagle's nest. In the background, you'll hear recorded birds' calls.

★ **Mendenhall Glacier:** It's little wonder that more than 250,000 tourists come to gawk at this glacier in Mendenhall Valley. It rises above the city like a leftover from the ice age. Walk down the paved trail or through a simulated ice cave. Take your turn looking through the huge glass windows for the perfect view.

Kayaking near Mendenhall Glacier

Klondike Gold Rush National Historical Park

## Skagway

★ **Klondike Gold Rush National Historical Park:** Step back in time and imagine the call of "Gold!" echoing down these streets and through the dozen restored historical buildings.

## Sitka

★ **Sitka National Historical Park:** Stand on the site of the 1804 Battle of Sitka, when Russian invaders took over the area from Tlingits. Examine the incredible totem poles and watch how Native Alaskan crafts are made as the people answer your questions about their history. In the evening, be sure to stay for a traditional Native Alaskan dance performance at the community house.

A California sea lion and zoo keeper at the Alaska Zoo

## SEE IT HERE!

### ALASKA RAPTOR CENTER

A favorite tourist destination is Sitka's Alaska Raptor Center. It is dedicated to rescuing and rehabilitating birds of prey—especially eagles. If birds can be healed, they may be able to go back to the wild. If they are too injured to survive on their own, they stay at the center where they help entertain more than 36,000 visitors or educate 15,000 schoolkids through classroom presentations.

## SOUTH-CENTRAL

**THINGS TO DO:** Listen to a storyteller, learn a craft, visit animals at a zoo, go mining for gold, and watch blue ice tumble off a glacier into the water.

### Anchorage

★ **The Alaska Native Heritage Center:** Here you'll learn about Alaska's first people and the rich heritage of the region's different cultural groups. The center offers school visits, lectures, classes, and workshops. You'll find out about Native traditions and customs of the past and present.

★ **Alaska Zoo:** Now that you've read about all the animals that live in Alaska, come and meet them for yourself at the zoo. You'll see polar bears and find out how global warming is affecting their habitat. The zoo is home to native species as well as some exotic creatures, such as snow leopards and elephants!

★ **Lake Hood:** Take off from the world's busiest seaplane airport for an eagle's-eye view of the state. Go flightseeing along the Alaska Range, over glaciers, and to Denali National Park.

### Girdwood

★ **Crow Creek Mine:** Step back in time at this still-active mine that dates to 1898. It's a great place to see what frontier life was like. Visitors can pan for gold, and everybody gets a bag of dirt with some gold in it.

## Valdez-Cordova Borough

★ **Child Glacier:** Head east from Cordova to visit Child Glacier, a 20-story-high glacier along the Copper River.

## Seward

★ **Alaska SeaLife Center:** If you can't visit the center in person, go to its Web site (www.alaskasea-life.org) where you can watch live video from Chiswell Island of Steller's sea lions. Visitors at the center will see fascinating Gulf of Alaska sea life, from puffins to harbor seals to giant Pacific octopuses! There's a touch tank where you can get up close and personal with a starfish. At the *Exxon Valdez* display, you'll see how devastating an oil spill can be.

Visitors at Alaska SeaLife Center

Aboard the *Klondike Express* in Prince William Sound

## Valdez

★ **Prince William Sound:** In the mood for a boat ride? On Prince William Sound there are plenty of tour boats at your service. You will see marine mammals and eagles in their natural habitats, awesome glaciers rising out of the water, and—if you time it just right—you might see chunks of ice tumble from the glaciers into the sea.

## Homer

★ **Visitor Center:** What's great about Homer? Stop by the Visitor Information Center and find out! Homer is a seaside community of 4,000 people overlooking Kachemak Bay and the Kenai Mountains. There are several exhibits at the center, and a film tells you about the people who work in Aleutian Island refuges.

Grizzly bears in Katmai National Park

## SOUTHWEST

**THINGS TO DO: Visit one of busiest bear refuges in the world, watch the annual salmon run, and see how a volcano changed the landscape.**

### King Salmon

★ **Katmai National Park:** Head here in July and September and watch fish leap out of the water like nowhere else in the world. So many fish course through the Brooks River that up to 60 brown bears come to the water's edge to gorge on fresh fish. Line up on the viewing platform and watch the salmon run!

★ **The Valley of Ten Thousand Smokes:** The largest volcanic eruption of the 20th century happened here in 1912. It turned a thriving forest into a desolate, treeless land. Steam and gas continued to escape from cracks in the ground for decades after, giving the valley its name.

### Kodiak Island

★ **Wildlife watching:** It may be beautiful here, but it's not a popular stop. Most of the island is a refuge for bears, and the visitors who do come by spend most of their time kayaking, fishing, and hiking.

# THE INTERIOR

**THINGS TO DO:** Head back to gold rush days, find out what it's like to live in a frigid climate, and join a square dance.

## Fairbanks

★ **Pioneer Park:** Visit a Native Alaskan village, climb aboard a restored steam locomotive, play a round of mini golf, or join in a square dance. You can do it all at Pioneer Park.

★ **Gold Rush Town:** Strolling through a town filled with buildings from the gold rush days will give you a sense of what life was like more than a century ago.

Tourists pan for gold

Climbers' campsite on a glacier in Denali National Park

★ **Fairbanks Ice Museum:** Grab your coat and walk into a freezer that is kept at −20°F (−29°C). Brrr! Check out the amazing ice sculptures before you head out for a cup of hot chocolate.

★ **Denali National Park:** Feeling adventurous? Take one of the park's bus rides. They can last up to eight hours, and both the magnificent scenery and the steep roads will take your breath away. The roads lack guardrails, so the trip may be a little too exciting for some. While on the bus, don't forget to look up and see Denali, the state's highest point.

## FAR NORTH

**THINGS TO DO: Keep warm!** It isn't always easy in these parts because this is the farthest north one can go and still be in the United States.

### Nome

★ **Seward Peninsula:** If you're feeling adventurous, rent a vehicle and explore the wilderness on your own. Birders, photographers, and wildlife enthusiasts consider this area to be paradise.

Battling the falls of Davis Creek in Seward Peninsula

★ **Bering Land Bridge National Preserve:** This preserve is named for the land link that once connected Alaska and Asia. This area is home to grizzly bears, reindeer, moose, and more than 170 species of birds. You can get there by small boat or small plane in the summer or by snowmobile, dogsled, or ski plane in the winter.

### Barrow

★ **Guided tours:** Don't try seeing this town on your own! Visitors take tours because in this city there is no downtown, and there are no cute souvenir shops, or even any obvious public places. Let the experts show you around. Most tours stop at the Inupiat Heritage Center, the town's main attraction. This is the only place in the United States where tourists can go on polar bear viewing tours!

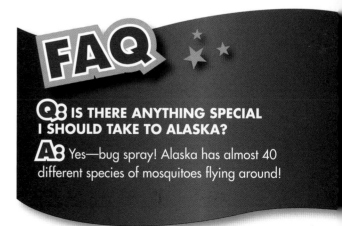

# FAQ

**Q: IS THERE ANYTHING SPECIAL I SHOULD TAKE TO ALASKA?**

**A:** Yes—bug spray! Alaska has almost 40 different species of mosquitoes flying around!

# SCIENCE, TECHNOLOGY, & MATH PROJECTS

Make weather maps, graph population statistics, and research endangered species that live in the state.

# PRIMARY VS. SECONDARY SOURCES

So what are primary and secondary sources? And what's the diff? This section explains all that and where you can find them.

# BIOGRAPHICAL DICTIONARY

This at-a-glance guide highlights some of the state's most important and influential people. Visit this section and read about their contributions to the state, the country, and the world.

# RESOURCES

Books, Web sites, DVDs, and more. Take a look at these additional sources for information about the state.

# WRITING PROJECTS

★ ★ ★

## Create an Election Brochure or Web Site!

**Run for office!**

Throughout this book you've read about some of the issues that concern Alaska today. As a candidate for governor of Alaska, create a campaign brochure or Web site.

★ Explain how you meet the qualifications to be governor of Alaska, and talk about the three or four major issues you'll focus on if you are elected.

★ Remember, you'll be responsible for Alaska's budget! How would you spend the taxpayers' money?

**SEE:** Chapter Seven, pages 89–97.

**GO TO:** Alaska's Government Web site at www.alaska.gov

## Write a Memoir, Journal, or Editorial for Your School Newspaper!

**Picture Yourself . . .**

★ As a U.S. senator debating the drilling for oil in wilderness areas. Would you be for it or against it? Why?

★ Building a umiak (boat) out of a tree. How long would it take, and what tools would you use?

★ As a dog musher in the Iditarod. What would a race day be like?

**SEE:** Chapters One, Two, and Six, pages 9–35 and 69–87.

## Compare and Contrast —When, Why, and How Did They Come?

Compare the migrations and explorations of Alaska's first Native people and its first European explorers. Tell about:

★ When their migrations began
★ How they traveled
★ Why they migrated
★ Where their journeys began and ended
★ What they found when they arrived

**SEE:** Chapters Two and Three, pages 27–43.

Native village

# ART PROJECTS

★ ★ ★

## Create a PowerPoint Presentation or Visitors' Guide

**Welcome to Alaska!**

Alaska's a great place to visit and to live! From its natural beauty to its historical sites, there's plenty to see and do. In your PowerPoint presentation or brochure, highlight 10 to 15 of Alaska's fascinating landmarks. Be sure to include:

★ a map of the state showing where these sites are located

★ photos, illustrations, Web links, natural history facts, geographic stats, climate and weather info, and descriptions of plants and animals

   **SEE:** Chapters One and Nine, pages 8–25 and 109–115.

   **GO TO:** The official Web site of Alaska tourism at www.travelalaska.com. Download and print maps, photos, national landmark images, and vacation ideas for tourists.

## Illustrate the Lyrics to the Alaska State Song

**("Alaska's Flag")**

Use markers, paints, photos, collage, colored pencils, or computer graphics to illustrate the lyrics to "Alaska's Flag," the state song! Turn your illustrations into a picture book, or scan them into a PowerPoint and add music!

**SEE:** The lyrics to "Alaska's Flag" on page 128.

**GO TO:** The Alaska state Web site at www.alaska.gov to find out more about the origin of the Alaska state song, "Alaska's Flag."

## Research Alaska's State Quarter

From 1999 to 2008, the U.S. Mint introduced new quarters commemorating each of the 50 states in the order that they were admitted to the Union. Each state's quarter features a unique design on its reverse, or back.

**GO TO:** www.usmint.gov/kids and find out what's featured on the back of the Alaska quarter.

Research and write an essay explaining:

★ the significance of each image

★ who designed the quarter

★ who chose the final design

Design your own Alaska state quarter. What images would you choose for the reverse?

★ Make a poster showing the Alaska quarter and label each image.

# SCIENCE, TECHNOLOGY, & MATH PROJECTS

★ ★ ★

## Graph Population Statistics!

★ Compare population statistics (such as ethnic background, birth, death, and literacy rates) in Alaska boroughs or major cities.

★ On your graph or chart, look at population density, and write sentences describing what the population statistics show; graph one set of population statistics, and write a paragraph explaining what the graphs reveal.

**SEE:** Chapter Six, pages 71–75.

**GO TO:** The official Web site for the U.S. Census Bureau at www.census.gov, and at http://quickfacts.census.gov/qfd/states/02000.html, to find out more about population statistics, how they work, and what the statistics are for Alaska.

## Create a Weather Map of Alaska!

Use your knowledge of Alaska's geography to research and identify conditions that result in specific weather events. What is it about the geography of Alaska that makes it vulnerable to things such as severe snowstorms? Create a weather map or poster that shows the weather patterns over the state. Include a caption explaining the technology used to measure weather phenomena, and provide data.

**SEE:** Chapter One, pages 17–19.

**GO TO:** The National Oceanic and Atmospheric Administration's National Weather Service Web site at www.weather.gov for weather maps and forecasts for Alaska.

Humpback whale

## Track Endangered Species

★ Using your knowledge of Alaska's wildlife, research which animals and plants are endangered or threatened. Find out what the state is doing to protect these species.

★ Chart known populations of the animals and plants, and report on changes in certain geographic areas

**SEE:** Chapter One, page 20.

**GO TO:** The U.S. Fish and Wildlife site at http://alaska.fws.gov/fisheries/endangered

# PRIMARY VS. SECONDARY SOURCES

★ ★ ★

## What's the Diff?

**Your teacher may require at least one or two primary sources and one or two secondary sources for your assignment. So what's the difference between the two?**

★ **Primary sources are original.** You are reading the actual words of someone's diary, journal, letter, autobiography, or interview. Primary sources can also be photographs, maps, prints, cartoons, news/film footage, posters, first-person newspaper articles, drawings, musical scores, and recordings. By the way, when you conduct a survey, interview someone, shoot a video, or take photographs to include in a project, you are creating primary sources!

★ **Secondary sources are what you find in encyclopedias, textbooks, articles, biographies, and almanacs.** These are written by a person or group of people who tell about something that happened to someone else. Secondary sources also recount what another person said or did. This book is an example of a secondary source.

## Now that you know what primary sources are—where can you find them?

★ **Your school or local library:** Check the library catalog for collections of original writings, government documents, musical scores, and so on. Some of this material may be stored on microfilm. The Library of Congress Web site (www.loc.gov) is an excellent online resource for primary source materials.

★ **Historical societies:** These organizations keep historical documents, photographs, and other materials. Staff members can help you find what you are looking for. History museums are also great places to see primary sources firsthand.

★ **The Internet:** There are lots of sites that have primary sources you can download and use in a project or assignment.

# TIMELINE

★  ★  ★

**U.S. Events** `1400` **Alaska Events**

**1492**
Christopher Columbus and his crew sight land in the Caribbean Sea.

`1600`

**1620**
Pilgrims found Plymouth Colony, the second permanent English settlement.

`1700`

Vitus Bering

**1728**
Vitus Bering sails through what becomes named the Bering Strait.

**1741**
Europeans arrive in Alaska.

**1776**
Thirteen American colonies declare their independence from Great Britain.

**1778**
Captain James Cook explores the Alaska area for Great Britain.

**1784**
The first Russian colony in North America is established at Three Saints Bay (now Kodiak).

**1787**
The U.S. Constitution is written.

`1800`

**1861–65**
The American Civil War is fought between the Northern Union and the Southern Confederacy; it ends with the surrender of the Confederate army, led by General Robert E. Lee.

**1867**
Russia sells Alaska to the United States.

**1863**
President Abraham Lincoln frees all slaves in the Southern Confederacy with the Emancipation Proclamation.

## U.S. Events

**1866**

The U.S. Congress approves the Fourteenth Amendment to the U.S. Constitution, granting citizenship to African Americans.

**1898**

The United States gains control of Cuba, Puerto Rico, the Philippines, and Guam after defeating Spain in the Spanish-American War.

**1917-18**

The United States engages in World War I.

**1920**

The Nineteenth Amendment to the U.S. Constitution grants women the right to vote.

**1929**

The stock market crashes, plunging the United States more deeply into the Great Depression.

**1941–45**

The United States engages in World War II.

**1951–53**

The United States engages in the Korean War.

## Alaska Events

A gold miner

**1889**

Thousands arrive in Alaska to search for gold.

**1899**

Railroad tycoon Edward Harriman leads an expedition to Alaska.

**1900**

The state capital moves from Sitka to Juneau.

**1914**

Congress authorizes the construction of the Alaska Railroad.

A railroad bridge

**1942**

The Japanese invade the Aleutian Islands.

**1959**

Alaska becomes the 49th state.

## U.S. Events

**1964–73**
The United States engages in the Vietnam War.

Trans-Alaska pipeline

**1991**
The United States and other nations engage in the brief Persian Gulf War against Iraq.

**2001**
Terrorists hijack four U.S. aircraft and crash them into the World Trade Center in New York City, the Pentagon in Arlington, Virginia, and a Pennsylvania field, killing thousands.

**2003**
The United States and Coalition forces invade Iraq.

## Alaska Events

**1964**
The Good Friday earthquake strikes.

**1977**
The Trans-Alaska pipeline is completed.

**1980**
President Jimmy Carter signs the Alaska National Interest Lands Conservation Act.

**1985**
The price of oil drops, hurting the Alaskan economy; many Alaskans leave the state.

**1989**
The *Exxon Valdez* spills oil in Prince William Sound.

A bird covered in oil after the Exxon Valdez spill

**2000**

**2001**
The governor issues the Millennium Agreement, agreeing to consult Native groups when making decisions.

**2005**
A track from 70-million-year-old dinosaur is found in Denali National Park.

**2006**
Alaska's first female governor takes office.

# GLOSSARY

**archaeologists** people who study the remains of past human societies

**boreal** of or belonging to the north

**canneries** factories where food is canned

**ecotourists** people who travel to a place to see unique natural sites

**epicenter** the focal or main point of an earthquake

**frostbite** partial freezing of parts of the body exposed to extreme cold

**glaciers** slow-moving masses of ice

**hypothermia** abnormally low body temperature that threatens a person's ability to function physically and mentally

**latitude** the position of a place, measured in degrees north or south of the equator

**magnitude** a mathematical scale to measure the strength of something

**missionaries** people who try to convert others to a religion

**naturalist** a person who studies natural history

**permafrost** a permanently frozen layer of soil

**pesticide** any chemical or biological agent used to kill plant or animal pests

**Richter scale** the scale developed to measure the strength of an earthquake

**scurvy** a disease resulting from a lack of vitamin C in the diet

**segregated** separated from others, according to race, class, ethnic group, religion, or other factors

**sinew** an inflexible cord or band of connective tissue that joins muscle to bone

**taiga** forests that are found in cold, wet climates only

**tundra** treeless plains

# FAST FACTS

## State Symbols

| | |
|---|---|
| **Statehood date** | January 3, 1959, the 49th state |
| **Origin of state name** | From the Aleut word *Aliasksha* meaning "mainland" or "land that is not an island" |
| **State capital** | Juneau |
| **State nickname** | Last Frontier, Land of the Midnight Sun |
| **State motto** | "North to the future" |
| **State bird** | Willow ptarmigan |
| **State flower** | Forget-me-not |
| **State fish** | King salmon |
| **State mineral** | Gold |
| **State gem** | Jade |
| **State insect** | Four-spot skimmer dragonfly |
| **State sport** | Dog mushing |
| **State song** | "Alaska's Flag" |
| **State tree** | Sitka spruce |
| **State fair** | Palmer (August–September) |

State seal

## Geography

| | |
|---|---|
| **Total area; rank** | 663,267 square miles (1,717,854 sq km); 1st |
| **Land; rank** | 571,951 square miles (1,481,347 sq km); 1st |
| **Water; rank** | 91,316 square miles (236,507 sq km); 1st |
| **Inland water; rank** | 17,243 square miles (44,659 sq km); 1st |
| **Coastal water; rank** | 27,049 square miles (70,057 sq km); 1st |
| **Territorial water; rank** | 47,024 square miles (121,792 sq km); 1st |
| **Geographic center** | 60 miles (97 km) northwest of Denali, 63° 50′ N, 152° W |
| **Latitude** | 54° 40′ N to 71° 50′ N |
| **Longitude** | 130° W to 173° E |
| **Highest point** | Denali, 20,320 feet (6,194 m) |
| **Lowest point** | Sea level along the Pacific Ocean |
| **Largest city** | Anchorage |
| **Organized boroughs** | 16 |

# Population

| | |
|---|---|
| **Population; rank (2006 estimate)** | 670,053; 47th |
| **Density (2006 estimate)** | 1 person per square mile (0.4 per sq km) |
| **Population distribution (2000 census)** | 66% urban, 34% rural |
| **Ethnic distribution (2005 estimate)** | White persons: 70.5%* |
| | American Indian and Alaska Native persons: 16.0%* |
| | Asian persons: 4.6%* |
| | Black persons: 3.7%* |
| | Native Hawaiian and Other Pacific Islander: 0.6%* |
| | Persons reporting two or more races: 4.7% |
| | Persons of Hispanic or Latino origin: 5.1%† |
| | White persons not Hispanic: 66.5% |

*Hispanics may be of any race, so they are also included in applicable race categories.*
*† Includes persons reporting only one race.*

# Weather

| | |
|---|---|
| **Record high temperature** | 100°F (38°C) at Fort Yukon on June 27, 1915 |
| **Record low temperature** | −80°F (−62°C) at Prospect Creek, near Stevens Village, on January 23, 1971 |
| **Average July temperature, Anchorage** | 58°F (14°C) |
| **Average January temperature, Anchorage** | 16°F (−9°C) |
| **Average July temperature, Barrow** | 40°F (4°C) |
| **Average January temperature, Barrow** | −14°F (−26°C) |
| **Average annual precipitation, Anchorage** | 16 inches (41 cm) |
| **Average annual precipitation, Barrow** | 4 inches (10 cm) |

State flag

# STATE SONG

★ ★ ★

## "Alaska's Flag"
Words by Marie Drake and music by Elinor Dusenbury

In 1935, Marie Drake, who worked for the Alaska Department of Education, wrote a poem about Benny Benson's flag for the cover of the *School Bulletin* newsletter. Later, Elinor Dusenbury set Drake's words to music, and in 1955, the song became the official territorial and then state song. A second verse was later written by Carol Beery Davis.

Eight stars of gold on a field of blue,
Alaska's Flag, may it mean to you
The blue of the sea, the evening sky,
The mountain lakes and the flow'rs nearby,
The gold of the early sourdough dreams,
The precious gold of the hills and streams,
The brilliant stars in the northern sky,
The Bear, the Dipper, and shining high,
The great North star with its steady light.
O'er land and sea a beacon bright,
Alaska's Flag to Alaskans dear,
The simple flag of a last frontier.

A Native lad chose the Dipper's stars
For Alaska's flag that there be no bars
Among our cultures. Be it known
Through years the Natives' past has grown
To share life's treasures, hand in hand,
To keep Alaska our Great Land;
We love the northern, midnight sky,
The mountains, lakes, and streams nearby.
The great North Star with its steady light
Will guide all cultures, clear and bright,
With nature's flag to Alaskans dear,
The simple flag of the last frontier.

# NATURAL AREAS AND HISTORIC SITES

★  ★  ★

## National Parks

Alaska has eight national parks, including *Gates of the Arctic National Park and Preserve*, *Glacier Bay National Park and Preserve*, *Katmai National Park and Preserve*, *Kenai Fjords National Park*, *Kobuk Valley National Park*, and *Lake Clark National Park and Preserve*. *Denali National Park and Preserve* contains Denali (Mount McKinley), North America's highest peak. *Wrangell-Saint Elias National Park and Preserve* is the largest unit in the national park system and includes three mountain ranges and many glaciers.

## National Preserves

Alaska is home to three national preserves. The *Bering Land Bridge National Preserve* is the remnant of the land bridge that connected North America to Asia more than 13,000 years ago. The *Noatak National Preserve* contains the largest mountain-ringed river basin in the United States and is still virtually untouched by humans. And the *Yukon–Charley Rivers National Preserve* protects part of the Yukon River and all of the Charley River basin.

## National Monuments

Alaska's two national monuments are the *Aniakchak National Monument*, which is a great volcanic crater that last erupted in 1931, and the *Cape Krusenstern National Monument*, which is an archaeological site containing evidence of 4,000 years of human habitation.

## National Historic Parks

Alaska showcases three national historic parks: the *Klondike Gold Rush National Historical Park*, which memorializes the 1897 gold rush; the *Sitka National Historical Park*, which is the site of a fort and the battle that was the last major resistance of the Tlingit people against Russian settlers; and the *Aleutian World War II National Historic Area*, which commemorates the Aleutian campaign of World War II.

## National Forests

Alaska has the nation's two largest national forests, the *Tongass National Forest*, which encompasses nearly 17 million acres (7 million ha), and the *Chugach National Forest*, which covers 5.5 million acres (2.2 million ha).

## State Parks and Forests

Alaska began establishing its state park system in the 1960s. Today, it includes 119 different parks, recreation areas, trails, and historic sites, including *Denali State Park*, located right next to *Denali National Park and Preserve*.

Denali National Park

# CULTURAL INSTITUTIONS

★ ★ ★

## Libraries

The *Alaska State Library* (Juneau) contains the state archives, as well as historical collections on Alaska's past.

The *University of Alaska Fairbanks,* the *University of Alaska Anchorage*, and the *University of Alaska Southeast* all have academic libraries.

## Museums

The *Alaska Museum of Natural History* (Anchorage) boasts the largest exhibits of rocks, minerals, and rare fossils in the state.

The *Alaska Native Heritage Center* (Anchorage) is an educational and cultural institution for all Alaskans that provides programs in both academic and informal settings, including workshops, demonstrations, and guided tours of indoor exhibits and outdoor village sites.

The *Alaska State Museum* (Juneau) contains exhibits and objects from Alaska Native cultures.

The *Alaska State Trooper Museum* (Anchorage) showcases the history of law enforcement in Alaska through exhibits, memorabilia, and photographs.

The *Anchorage Museum at the Rasmuson Center* (Anchorage) features exhibits and collections representing Alaska Natives, Alaska history, and Alaskan art.

The *Juneau-Douglas City Museum* (Juneau) features exhibits and videos that highlight early Juneau life and gold-mining history.

The *Last Chance Mining Museum* (Juneau) features one of the world's largest air compressors and other industrial artifacts associated with hard-rock gold mining.

The *Sheldon Jackson Museum* (Sitka) has Alaska Native collections.

The *University of Alaska Museum of the North* (Fairbanks) contains historical and wildlife exhibits, as well as a collection of Alaskan art.

## Performing Arts

Alaska has one major opera company.

## Universities and Colleges

As of 2006, Alaska had ten public and four private institutions of higher learning.

# ANNUAL EVENTS

## January–March

**Russian Christmas** in cities across the state (early January)

**Winter Sunrise** in Barrow (late January)

**Fur Rendezvous** in Anchorage (February)

**Iditarod Trail Sled Dog Race** (March)

**Pillar Mountain Golf Classic** in Kodiak (March)

## April–June

**Alaska Folk Festival** in Juneau (April)

**Jazz and Classics Festival** in Juneau (May)

**Little Norway Festival** in Petersburg (May)

**Kodiak Crab Festival** (May)

**The Midnight Sun** in Barrow (mid-May)

**Sitka Summer Music Festival** (June)

## July–September

**World Eskimo-Indian Olympics** in Fairbanks (July)

**State Fair** in Palmer (August–September)

**Equinox Marathon** in Fairbanks (September)

## October–December

**Alaska Day Celebration** in Sitka, commemorating the transfer of Alaska from Russia to the United States in 1867 (October)

**Athabascan Fiddling Festival** in Fairbanks (November)

**Great Alaska Shootout** in Anchorage, featuring college basketball teams from throughout the United States (November)

Senior Native Youth Olympic Games

# BIOGRAPHICAL DICTIONARY

**Alexandr Baranov** See page 46.

**E. L. "Bob" Bartlett (1904–1968)** was a congressman from Alaska. He grew up in Fairbanks and fought hard for statehood.

**Irene Bedard** See page 81.

**Benny Benson (1913–1972)** designed the Alaskan state flag at age 13. He was born in Chignik.

**Vitus Bering** See page 39.

**Ada Blackjack** See page 22.

**Carlos Boozer Jr. (1981–)** is an NBA basketball player who has played for the Cleveland Cavaliers and the Utah Jazz. Born on a military base in Germany, he grew up in Juneau.

**Susan Butcher (1954–2006)** is the only woman to have won the Iditarod four times: in 1986, 1987, 1988, and 1990. In 1989, she came in second and was in the top five finishers a dozen times. She was born in Boston.

Carlos Boozer

**James Cook** See page 42.

**William Egan** See page 92.

**Carl Ben Eielson (1897–1929)** was a pilot who made the first Alaska airmail flight in 1924. It took him four hours to go from Fairbanks to McGrath, a trip that would have taken dogsleds 20 days. He was born in North Dakota.

**Scott Gomez (1979–)** was the National Hockey League's Rookie of the Year in 2000. He was born in Anchorage.

Scott Gomez

Susan Butcher

**George T. Harper** See page 61.

**Michael A. Healy (1839–1904)** was a coast Guard officer who served in Alaskan waters. Born in Macon, Georgia, he helped improve living conditions for the territory's Native people.

**Molly Hootch (1960–)** was one of the students who sued the Alaska Board of Education and ensured that Alaskan villages had high schools. She was born in Nunapitchuk.

**Jewel Kilcher** See page 79.

Michael Healy

**Trajan Langdan (1976–)** is a professional basketball player who has played for the Cleveland Cavaliers and for international teams. He was born in Anchorage.

**Austin Eugene Lathrop** See page 105.

**Hilary Lindh (1969–)** is a 1992 Olympic medal winner in downhill skiing. She was born in Juneau.

Hilary Lindh

Trajan Langdon

Jack London

**Jack London (1876–1916)** was an author who wrote *Call of the Wild* and many other books. He was born in San Francisco but spent much time in Alaska.

**Ray Mala (1906–1952)** was one of the first successful Native Alaskan actors of his era. Born in Alaska Territory, he starred in more than 25 films.

**Tommy Moe (1970–)** won two Olympic medals for downhill skiing in 1994. Born in Montana, he trained in Alaska.

**Dorothy Page (1921–1989)** is remembered as the Mother of the Iditarod. From 1973 to 1989, she wrote, edited, and published the Iditarod's annual race program, and she edited the *Iditarod Runner*. She also served as mayor of Wasilla for two years. She was born in New Mexico but moved to Alaska in 1960.

**Sarah Palin** See page 94.

**Virgil Partch (1916–1984)** was a cartoonist at Walt Disney Studios and the creator of the character "Big George." He was born on St. Paul Island.

**Elizabeth Wanamaker Peratrovich**
See page 62.

Elizabeth Wanamaker Peratrovich

**Joe Redington Sr. (1917–1999)** is remembered as the Father of the Iditarod. He participated in the Iditarod a number of times, finishing in the top five at age 71. He was born in Oklahoma but moved to Alaska in 1948.

**Libby Riddles (1956–)** was the first woman to win the Iditarod. Born in Wisconsin, she became a dog breeder and wrote books about her Alaskan adventures.

Libby Roderick

**Libby Roderick (1958–)** is a singer and songwriter who was born in Anchorage. She is also an activist who speaks out on Native American issues.

**Leohnard Seppala (1877–1966)** was a dogsled racer who raced medicine to Nome in 1925 to help prevent a diphtheria outbreak. He was born in Norway.

**Deb Vanasse** See page 80.

**Ivan Veniaminov** See page 48.

**Velma Wallis (1960–)** is an author who writes about Alaska. She was born in Fort Yukon.

Libby Riddles

Deb Vanasse

# RESOURCES

★ ★ ★

## BOOKS

### Nonfiction

Belarde-Lewis, Miranda. *Meet Lydia: A Native Girl from Southeast Alaska*. Tulsa: Council Oak Books, 2004.

Brown, Tricia. *Children of the Midnight Sun: Young Native Voices of Alaska*. Portland, Ore.: Alaska Northwest Books, 2006.

Corral, Kimberly. *My Denali: Exploring Alaska's Favorite National Park with Hannah Corral*. Portland, Ore.: Alaska Northwest Books, 1995.

Dolan, Ellen M. *Susan Butcher and the Iditarod Race*. New York: Walker, 1996.

Haycox, Stephen. *Alaska: An American Colony*. Seattle: University of Washington Press, 2002.

Niz, Xavier. *Alaska (Land of Liberty)*. Mankato, Minn.: Capstone Press, 2003.

Pascoe, Elaine. *Into Wild Alaska: The Jeff Corwin Experience*. San Diego: Blackbirch Press, 2004.

Weber, Jen F. *Clueless in Alaska: Know More! An Activity Book Filled with Puzzles, Fun Facts, Games and Jokes*. Seattle: Sasquatch Books, 2006.

### Fiction

Granum, Hal. *The Great Eagle Spirit*. Frederick, Md.: PublishAmerica, 2006.

London, Jack. *Call of the Wild*. New York: Scholastic, 2001.

Napoli, Donna Jo. *North*. New York: HarperTrophy, 2006.

O'Dell, Scott. *Black Star, Bright Dawn*. New York: Fawcett, 1989.

Vanasse, Deb. *A Distant Enemy*. New York: Dutton, 1997.

Vanasse, Deb. *Out of the Wilderness*. New York: Clarion, 1999.

Wallis, Velma. *Bird Girl and the Man Who Followed the Sun*. New York: Harper Perennial, 1997.

Wallis, Velma. *Two Old Women: An Alaska Legend of Courage, Betrayal and Survival*. New York: Harper Perennial, 2004.

# DVDs

*Alaska: Spirit of the Wild.* Razor, 2005.
*Alaska's Inside Passage.* Questar, 2005.
*Building the Alaska Highway* (American Experience). PBS, 2005.
*Denali: Alaska's Great Wilderness* (The Living Edens). PBS, 2005.
*Glaciers: Alaska's Rivers of Ice.* DVD International, 2003.
*The Great Alaska Train Adventure* (America's Scenic Rail Journeys). Acorn Media, 2000.
*National Parks of Alaska.* Image Entertainment, 2002.
*Over Alaska.* KCTS Television, 2001.

# WEB SITES AND ORGANIZATIONS

### Alaska Department of Natural Resources

*www.dnr.state.ak.us/parks/*
This site has information about Alaska's parks and outdoor recreation.

### Alaska Division of Tourism

*www.travelalaska.com*
Visit this site to learn about great activities and attractions throughout the state.

### Alaska Humanities Forum

*www.akhistorycourse.org*
This site provides varied facts and viewpoints about Alaskan history and culture.

### Alaska Museum of Natural History

*www.alaskamuseum.org*
This site gives details about the latest exhibits.

### Alaska Volcano Observatory

*www.avo.alaska.edu*
You can learn about the state's hazardous volcanoes at this site.

### The Alaska Zoo

*www.alaskazoo.org*
Take an online tour of this remarkable collection of animals.

### State of Alaska

*www.state.ak.us*
This site explains how the government works and provides links to various departments and agencies.

# INDEX

★ ★ ★

# AUTHOR'S TIPS AND SOURCE NOTES

★ ★ ★

While researching this book, I learned that during the northern lights, if you are really still, you can hear them crackle as the hairs go up on the back of your neck.

To learn about Alaska, my family and I vacationed there. I also read lots of books and watched several videos. *The Reader's Companion to Alaska* by Alan Ryan is a great resource, as is *The Native People of Alaska* by Steve J. Langdon. I spent a huge amount of time online. The Alaska Historical Society Web site (www.alaskahistoricalsociety.org) had loads of information, and I found wonderful visitors' information at www.travelalaska.com. It's easy to see why tourists like Alaska so much. There is something for everyone in a land this big.